Colin Odell & Michelle Le Blanc

The Pocket Essential

HORROR FILMS

www.pocketessentials.com

First published in Great Britain 2001 by Pocket Essentials, 18 Coleswood Road, Harpenden, Herts, AL5 1EQ

Distributed in the USA by Trafalgar Square Publishing, PO Box 257, Howe Hill Road, North Pomfret, Vermont 05053

A CIP catalogue record for this book is available from the British Library.

ISBN 1-903047-38-2

9 8 7 6 5 4 3 2 1

Book typeset by Pdunk
Printed and bound by Cox & Wyman

For Alice, our little horror

Acknowledgements

Er, normally at this stage we thank lots of people for lending us resource materials but we seem to be such reprobates that our collection spoke for itself. Thanks to our parents who thoroughly disapprove of all the nasty films we watch and Marc, who thoroughly approves of the films we watch. Thanks also to Paul Duncan, Steve Holland and Elizabeth Billinger. A big hello to Tony, Andy, Lizbeth, Paul, Gary, Kay, Elyse and Jim on the Camera Obscurer web bounce. To Flo and Mo, who stalk the fields of Alderney and finally to Alice, who tortures and kills small furry creatures and leaves their remains on the carpet...

CONTENTS

Introduction

What Is Horror?

A fork of lightning traverses the moonless sky, briefly illuminating an inhuman shape crouched before the fragile window pane. With the wooden shutters banging in the screeching wind and the floorboards creaking under some unseen strain you swear you can hear the sound of unfamiliar footsteps and something scraping along the ancient walls like fingernails slowly being dragged along a blackboard...

Despite its reputation as lowbrow or mindless entertainment the horror film has a rich literary and oral tradition that eclipses many other forms of storytelling. Primarily, confrontation of fear in a safe environment (whether it's in a cinema, around a campfire or snuggled up in bed) works at a primordial level to psychologically prepare an individual for life's hardships as well as acting as a cautionary source of morality. To this end, the best tales are told in the dark or at night where the logical light of day cannot disperse their phantasmagorical effect or mock their inherently dubious premises. Ultimately, the horror film is a faerie or folk story, no different to Grimm's traditional oral tales, just presented to the audience in a manner suited to our times. Throughout history, humankind has been fascinated by the bizarre, the macabre and the horrific - from revelling in ancient gladiatorial battles to modern motorists gawping at an accident, terror has always formed a part of our lives. The horror film offers a chance to experience this fear and disgust within a fantastical and physically non-threatening context. There is a catharsis within horror - to see victims deal with a situation, jump at the scary moments and recoil at the grotesque, but ultimately leave the cinema unscathed. It also offers an ideal date setting, which is why it is so popular with teens - a scary movie is just the thing to ensure that you both cuddle up close.

Other precedents for the horror film come from the work of artists such as Bruegel, Bosch or the surrealists, the sublime canvases of the late 18th century or the distorted realities of Hogarth. Mix this with psychoanalysis and centuries of esoteric underground thinking and the resulting concoction is a miasma of subgenres and styles that make the horror film an incredibly rich part of cinema's heritage. However, they are often simply dismissed as trash or unworthy of serious critical attention. Thomas Schatz's seminal work on Hollywood genres does not even acknowledge the horror film, yet imbues the Western with a sense of mythicism, and despite some attempt to address the issue, horror remains the province of the fan rather than the critic. Despite (or because of) this, its continued popularity indicates that people will part with their money time and again for the privilege of being scared witless, just as they have from the start of cinema and storytelling itself.

Order - Chaos - Reconstruction

The basic structural premise of the horror film is to show the restoration or reconstruction of an order in a portrayed society. The opening act (ignoring prologues which are designed to create tension or provide justification for the disruption of order) generally sets the groundwork for a community unaware of impending danger, either a 'normal town' (*Halloween, Gremlins*), an isolated group (*The Thing, Deliverance, Friday The Thirteenth*) or an individual (*Carrie, The Vanishing*). The second act sees the arrival of the monster, the breakdown of social order and change, the prologue often gives a portent of this act (*Halloween, Jaws, Friday The Thirteenth*). The final act resolves the issues, however swiftly, and restores order to the community, which may be different from the order that opened the picture. Most films follow this three-act structure although some, notably during the Sixties and Seventies, try to break from it by employing downbeat endings (*Night Of The Living Dead, The Birds*) that offer no solution to the problem, effectively ending in Act 2. But even these have an abrupt internal resolution (the absence of audience identifiable characters in *Night Of The Living Dead*, the probably temporary escape from *The Birds*). Some films play with the template - *Dawn Of The Dead* is set entirely in Act 2 but internally follows the three-act structure. The reconstruction of order does not necessarily mean that the new world is any better than the one that preceded it and is often far worse (*Invasion Of The Body Snatchers*) but its alteration and the process of reconstruction is what provides the genre's basic narrative drive.

The Monster

At the rotten core of any horror lies the monster, the perpetrator of the dread and fear that elicits an emotional response to the film. The monster need not be the obvious lumbering killer and neither does it follow that a killer in a film must be the monster, the purpose is to provide a reason for the chaos inflicted on the portrayed society. The monster falls into at least one, often more, of four basic categories which typify the disruption of order.

Natural: Nature is a primal fear, it is chaotic, unpredictable and often as violent as it is beautiful. Man's insignificance in the universe is epitomised by futile attempts at controlling the forces of nature. The greatest fear is that which we cannot understand and nature is the first manifestation of this. The ecological horror film shows the effects of nature on humankind, either as punishment for meddling with it (with which it is crossed with the scientific monster - e.g. the electrically awoken worms of *Squirm* or the genetics tampering of *Piranha* or *Jurassic Park*), the primitive attacking the modern upsetting the balance of evolution (*Jaws, Grizzly*), or the man as insignificant to the greater purpose of nature's slow cycle (*Volcano, Armageddon*). Resolution in the natural horror film is often by scientific means (*The Swarm*), confrontation which re-establishes the protagonist's link with his/her primitive self (*Jaws, Moby Dick*) or by nature just running its course (*Earthquake*).

Supernatural: In some respects, the supernatural offers a much safer form of horror. Although not tangible or simple to explain, it is far easier to dismiss as fantastical because cold logic requires empirical evidence of supernatural activity outside the cinematic environment. Ultimately the monster is a fantastical bogeyman that cannot rationally exist and can therefore be dismissed. Vampires, werewolves and zombies allow the audience to have their cake and eat it - they can enjoy the scares then dismiss the monster at their leisure. Conversely supernatural monsters, because of their unfathomable and enigmatic nature, allow the imaginative film-maker to create horror and terror extended outside our waking reality. Clive Barker's Cenobites (*Hellraiser*) come from a twisted, distorted world far beyond our comprehension. Supernatural creatures can come from anywhere and for any purpose, whether it be vampires taking over the world (*Blade*) or motiveless demonic possession (*The Exorcist, Stigmata*).

Psychological: Perhaps one of the most terrifying of monsters, the psychotic killer is based entirely in the real world. Sometimes these monsters are given an excuse, a reason for their actions - whether it be abuse at the hands of the father (*Peeping Tom*), a frightening Oedipal complex (*Maniac, Psycho*), a lost love - or are simply driven to madness by such mundane entities as noisy neighbours (*Driller Killer*). In these cases the audience may not be able to identify with the monster, but can at least understand it. Occasionally there is no obvious cause or explanation for a killer's crimes (*The Texas Chainsaw Massacre, Henry Portrait Of A Serial Killer*) or the malevolent motivation of a killer wanting simply to know how it feels to kill (*The Vanishing*) - the consequent alienation of the audience produces far more scary and sinister effects. These monsters are difficult to dismiss. Today's sensationalist press turn real life crimes into hard-hitting stories that ultimately exploit the victims, but their effect on the public psyche is hard to ignore. It is only when crossed with the supernatural that these killers become easier to deal with (*Halloween*).

Scientific: The reality of man-made disasters (plane crashes, Chernobyl) delivers a genuine threat to the audience. Many disaster movies of the Seventies (*The Towering Inferno, Airplane*) reflect very real threats that could "happen to anyone." Another genre favourite is the mad scientist, knowledgeable beyond everyday comprehension and fanatically driven that can lead to all sorts of evil, whether it be accidental or intentional. Dr Jekyll, Dr X, Fu Manchu, Professor Quatermass all created, in some sense, terrifying offspring of science. Frankenstein's monster is a product of a man's obsessive determination to create life from dead flesh, but who is really the monster - the creation or the creator? Concerns about the threat of the atom bomb and the destruction of the world through the clinical and relentless pursuit of science, for example the atomic mutation film, are further examples.

The Viewer: Voyeur, Victim, Violator

The complex relationship between viewer and screen provides a variety of conflicts for the spectator that go towards creating the style of a particular horror film. Horror is not the only genre to do this, but the way in which the viewpoints are mixed dictates the overall feel and makes the film horrific. The three primary modes of audience relationship to the screen are: Voyeur, Victim, Violator.

Voyeur: The privileged viewer can watch the acts of terror detached from the proceedings. The enjoyment lies in the spectacle or the relaying of the story. This can create tension in that the advantaged viewpoint allows us to see a killer waiting patiently at the side of the room (*Halloween*), the victim unaware of his presence. Linked with voyeurism is a scopophilic urge relating to the events and a helplessness that derives from being outside narrative intervention. Conversely, the detached viewpoint can result in a disinterested attitude, which allows the audience the luxury of viewing the film at an aesthetic level whilst removing the personal attachment to the characters. Although this position is generally undesirable in a horror film there are exceptions - in Jörg Buttgereit's *Der Todesking* this aesthetic distancing pushes matters into the arena of the art film and makes the morbid events non-exploitational.

Victim: Empathy with the character and experiencing the action from their point of view occasionally leaves the viewer the victim of the horror.

While the advantaged viewpoint leaves the spectator helpless, there is at least no direct threat, but from the victim's point of view this is not the case. In *The Texas Chainsaw Massacre* when Sally regains consciousness we watch (as she does) the ogling faces of the cannibal family who have captured her. In some sense we become her for that moment.

Violator: The camera as killer is a popular component of the horror film from Michael Powell's *Peeping Tom* to *Halloween* and *Wolfen*. The viewer sees as the killer and becomes implicit in the perpetration of the atrocity. This aspect has created much of the outrage against stalk 'n' slash films of the early Eighties, when it was argued that viewing through the killers' eyes reinforced the misogynist attitudes of these pictures and somehow encouraged the spectator to align with this way of thinking.

These three devices do not necessarily remain isolated. In John McNaughton's remarkable *Henry: Portrait Of A Serial Killer* the two killers, Henry and Otis, abuse and butcher a family. We see the scene, without cuts, from the point of view of a camcorder that is recording the slaughter, initially as violator (the camera begins as handheld) before becoming detached voyeur (as the camera is abandoned so its operator can indulge in violation). Sometimes all three techniques are used simultaneously (although rarely) such as in the prom massacre sequence in Brian De Palma's *Carrie* - the scene is played in split-screen so we simultaneously view the carnage from afar, from Carrie's viewpoint (glancing off one part of the screen another camera whip blurs to represent her viewpoint) and from her victims' perspective. Knowingly cinematic, the result makes the viewer at once voyeur, victim and violator.

The Scare And The Thrill

As with all films, the director and editor have complete control over what is revealed to the audience and when, but with horror this is key to generating tension and pacing. It is often true that the viewer's imagination provides far more scares than is possible for a film-maker to depict – the unseen can be any number of fears or phobias, personal to the individual. It is the reason many of horror's detractors have never seen a horror film - their anxiety lies with what they may see.

Editing is the main device which creates the pace of a film, compressing or extending time to accentuate the appropriate mood. There are fundamental differences between tension, suspense and shock. Hitchcock used suspense in films that would not normally be considered horror pictures but the effect remains the same. The device relies on giving the audience more information than the character has, then progressing with the plot while the

11

audience wait for the revelation/event - e.g. showing a character being given a bomb and waiting for it to explode or not, aligning the viewer to a subjectively omnipotent position. Tension is created by giving the audience a hint of what could happen, but not letting on when or how. Horror films tend to play tension one of two ways - the first is to slowly build the horror, dropping clues and subtle hints, each confrontation becoming nastier right up to the final showdown. The other device is completely opposite - show all the nastiness right at the start of the film and confront the audience head on. There is no need to show further terror, because the tension is established - the audience know how nasty things can get, but are still completely in the dark as to how much worse it can be. Shock lies the realm of the unexpected surprise, occasionally preceded by tension but distinct from it. Red herrings are, naturally, obligatory in most productions - why go for a complicated scare when a false alarm is just as effective? There is a term for this known as 'the bus' which derives from Jacques Tourneur's *Cat People*. After an interminably tense walk through a park, the hiss of bus brakes concludes the scene with safety for the character - a massive shock for the audience who have expected the worst. Similar uses are made of cats (Jones in *Alien* being the quintessential feline example) or, popular in many modern horrors, the two people bumping into each other in a school corridor, always accompanied by an accentuating musical 'dah-dah!'

How To Use This Book

First we look at the history of the horror film from its inception to the present day, giving an overview of the basic movements and looking at key films in more detail. Then we examine ten people who have a reputation for producing horror films, key movers in the field. We look at their lives, films and influences. Naturally we could not hope to cover the scale and number of horror films in a book of this size and sadly many classic films have been reluctantly omitted, notably those outside Europe or Hollywood, so your safety from Japanese ghosts, Chinese hopping vampires and Mexican monsters is assured. Instead we have attempted to provide a rough guide to a horror excursion, a package holiday, where you can take in all the major scare cities and sightsee in a couple of backwater villages of interest. If you enjoy your whirlwind stay you can always come back and explore some of the multitude of areas in more detail. Enjoy your horror holiday, it could be your last...

Silents Are Golden

The horror film, the shock picture, is such a disreputable form that it has been around since the dawn of cinema. Even before the development of narrative cinema, the horror film had already thrilled and chilled audiences. Georges Méliès, the pioneer of camera trickery, made many short films that had supernatural or macabre punchlines; from films about Faust, through a number of 'magic' illusions where Méliès himself would transform people into skeletons or inflate a head until it popped. The medium naturally progressed into the arena of storytelling. The Edison-produced *Frankenstein* (1910) is an early example and is thought to be the first appearance of the scientist's monster. Around this time protests about the effects of screen violence on the viewer were beginning to take hold, and have never stopped. After a few years as a novelty, cinema became a regular part of people's lives but, importantly, those people were generally working-class. While the Russian film industry grew with the realisation that film could be used as a powerful propaganda tool, elsewhere it was viewed with suspicion - an irresponsible medium for depraving the innocent mind. Some early examples of the kind of film that provoked such outrage now seem funny - the car running over a man's legs that then get detached is so ineptly executed (by today's standards) the howls are now of laughter, but there was a darker side too. Many successful early films depicted executions or 'foreign' atrocities, what we now call mondo movies, and their popularity caused such concern that they provided the opportunity to ban other material as well, including fictionalised sex and violence.

The first accepted classic of the genre was *The Cabinet Of Dr Caligari* - ironic in that many contemporary reviews dismissed the film as crude and sensationalist. Germany became the premiere producer of horror films, their very silence making them marketable the world over. The use of expressionist lighting and huge sets would have an enormous impact on the future of the field - these films dealt with fractured psychoses, distorted reality and emphasis on dreamtime. *Der Golem* (1920, there had been previous versions) makes full use of its locations as a clay creature is summoned, goes on a rampage but ultimately falls foul of an innocent little girl. In a poignant moment she casually removes the Golem's 'heart' in an influential scene reflected many years later in James Whale's *Frankenstein*. *Nosferatu* (1922), Murnau's unofficial adaptation of Bram Stoker's *Dracula* remains a masterpiece of vampire cinema, a taut, surreal and foetid exploration with a truly revolting monster (played by Max Schreck), driven by inhuman love. Murnau would go on to direct *Faust* (1926), a reworking of the famous legend about a man who sells his soul to Mephistopheles, before moving on to non-genre projects. Fritz Lang gave us a series of films based on the sinister Dr Mabuse, but remains chiefly remembered for the complex and disturbing *M* (1931), starring Peter Lorre as a child murderer. It was based on Peter Kurten, the Vampire of Düsseldorf - a brute whose legacy was still in the memories of contemporary viewers. Germany was not the only country making horror films. Hungary had been scaring audiences from word go and both French and English productions, especially in weekly part works, emphasised sensational and supernatural elements in their regular line up, in the literary shadow of Sax Rohmer. Scandinavian cinema was also very well regarded at the time.

On the other side of the Atlantic Hollywood had not remained idle. Lon Chaney terrified audiences the world over with his remarkable self applied make-up in films such as *The Hunchback Of Notre Dame* (1923) and *The Phantom Of The Opera* (1925). *London After Midnight* (1927) featured Chaney as a vampire, complete with painfully wired jaw and rows of sharpened teeth. John Barrymore excelled as *Dr Jekyll And Mr Hyde* (1920), but the film came under criticism for its brutality - the scene where he clubs a stranger to death is still shocking and sees echoes in the tramp killing sequence of Kubrick's *A Clockwork Orange* (1971). It also features a truly creepy sequence where a giant spider is superimposed crouching over a bed.

Silent cinema's legacy was that it provided a visual reference for future film-makers, relying on image to tell the story. By the close of the Twenties the level of technology and skill was phenomenal, creating some of the most potent images of international cinema. The coming of sound created a decline in non-English speaking movie cultures. But there was another bugbear around the corner to burden the unwary film-maker. Spurred by adverse press reaction to the effects of media violence and lascivious depictions of sexual promiscuity, Hollywood took it upon itself to clean up its act, before someone else did. England had already instigated a series of regulations in the shape of the BBFC but it was the Hays Code that would cripple artistic freedom. Initiated in the mid-Twenties no one took much notice initially, but by the mid-Thirties its Draconian edicts would see the beginning of a decline in the sensationalist horror picture. In some ways its effects are still being felt today.

The Cabinet Of Dr Caligari (1919)

Dir: Robert Weine St: Werner Krauss, Conrad Veidt

At Holstenwall fair, Dr Caligari introduces Cesare, a somnambulist who is kept in a coffin-like box and fed porridge by day. But by night Cesare does Caligari's insidious bidding, murdering or hypnotising townsfolk for his own nefarious purposes, and it seems as though nothing can stop him.

A defining moment in cinema's expression as an art form this was, at the time, passed off as a stagy and unrealistic amateur nasty. *Caligari* rejects any concept of realism in favour of a warped and fragmented version of psychological or dream reality - the world seen through the eyes of a madman telling a tale of unimaginable horrors. The incredible expressionist backdrops and imaginative set design conspire to make the entire experience disjointed; the mountainside is jam-packed with curvy triangular houses, Caligari's caravan is buckled, the clerks' chairs are imposing, while the streets are serpentine in their undulating cobbles. The fair is domineering and claustrophobic, its merry-go-round at a skewed angle, spinning so fast it shouldn't work. That these remarkable scenes are bookended by apparently normal moments in a lunatic asylum gives credence to their illusory nature, but this fantasy world invades the asylum itself - the inmates apparently connected by strings like human marionettes, overseen by their own Caligari. It is as though this world is no more real than the tale we have been told. Cesare may well kill Alan and stumble to the rooftops with the swooning hypnotised girl but he is a pawn, as is everyone else, to the dictatorial Caligari. Despite its poor initial reception the influence of this film is immense; the whole German expressionist movement that defined Europe's finest silent horrors owe a debt to Caligari's visual stylisation. Its combination of art and pulp psychology is what makes the film so watchable. Its influence spreads out to Terence Fisher's (c.f.) *Frankenstein And The Monster From Hell, The Crow* (1994) and most notably in the works of Tim Burton. Cesare is visually very much a precursor to *Edward Scissorhands* (1990) while much of the distorted set work can be seen in *The Nightmare Before Christmas* (Selick, 1993) and *Sleepy Hollow* (1999).

Haxan: A History Of Witchcraft Through The Ages (1921)

Dir: Benjamin Christensen

Doing exactly as its title suggests, Christensen's film shows the history and development of witchcraft, images of the devil and persecution through the ages, sparing none of the details and remaining refreshingly frank in its tone. Starting as a lecture, the factual tone does much to dissipate fears that this is an exploitation piece. To illustrate the world as seen in the middle ages, the film branches out into an animated illustration of the heavens before plunging into an awe-inspiring mechanical realisation of a Boschian Hell with endless bodies being devoured by demons and queues of people shuffling towards eternal torment. These images of mechanical grotesquery would later find good home in the macabre animations of Jan Svankmajer, whose aggressive animation style can also be seen in a breathtaking sequence of self-arranging coins. If that were not enough, the screen is set alight with dramatic reconstructions, proving to be far more than merely illustrative. We see the Devil in his many guises from towering obese horned priest, to sprightly Pan-clone and scaly beast, with a constantly twitching forked tongue. These are remarkable creations of makeup and acting; Maleus Maleficarum or Bosch brought to life. Neither is he portrayed as a bit evil or a touch of a scallywag. The debasement of the early texts is shown in full - a line of witches joyfully kissing his anus, corrupting a convent or tempting monks to sex and their masters to enjoy flagellation. The Sabbath sequence is the most renowned and controversial in the film. Following the witches from their homes the sky is filled with broom-riding women, capes fluttering, descending on a graveyard. There they meet dancing demons, the whole event overseen by Satan himself, clutching an unchristened baby from whom he squeezes the life blood and tosses into a bubbling cauldron.

But the demons aren't restricted to Satan's side, the damaging effects of the inquisition and religious fanaticism are also examined in sobering detail. The systematic torture and executions of (mainly) women at the hands of the inquisitors is dramatised and illustrated with reconstructions of the use of torture instruments designed to extract 'confessions' from unfortunate souls. If the film does have a failing it lies within the final section's need to rationalise 'witchly' behaviour in terms of psychoanalytic theories on hysteria but this is a minor point. Overall, this remains an affecting, fascinating, insightful work that manages to merge fact and the fantastical. Three years in the making the camerawork, giddying special effects and sensitive use of colour tinting make for a unique experience. If possible seek out the full print rather than the truncated one with narration by William Burroughs.

The Phantom Of The Opera (1925)

Dir: Rupert Julian St: Lon Chaney

Deep in the catacombs below the Paris Opera lurks a hideous, vengeful madman. He is Erik, the Phantom of the Opera. He does have a taste for music though and exercises his powers of persuasion to ensure that Christine Daaé gets prima donna status in the opera's production of Faust, providing she dedicates her life to her career and ditches her boyfriend Raoul. But when she fails to attain the Phantom's exacting demands, he decides to bring the house down. Literally.

Gaston Leroux's novel has had a long run on the big screen. The combination of grand scale, doomed twisted love, greed for the stage and a backdrop of decadent Paris is irresistible, providing the perfect grandiose melodrama and glut of scale that typifies both Opera and Hollywood big budget film-making. We are in big set territory here - the opera house is huge, the stage filled to the brim with ballerinas, wire work angels and trapdoors. The audience stampede in terror as they flee the giant chandelier crashing down upon them. The attention to design is second to none; sets of Faustian Hells in the wings, the Phantom's abode, from his austere coffin to Christine's boudoir, the black lake with its domineering arches traversed by means of gondolier, and the statue-dominated rooftops. In one of the film's most celebrated scenes the huge staircase of the foyer is the setting for the decadent Bal Masqué de l'Opéra, where the Phantom makes his presence felt as a skull-faced figure of death resplendent in a crimson cloak. To add greater impact and gravitas, the scene was originally shot in two-strip colour which emphasises the opulence. Despite the Phantom's obvious negative points (he's barking mad and homicidal) he still manages to come across as a figure of some sympathy; he is after all, in love, genuinely believing that its redemptive powers will dissipate his hatred for mankind. He is also self-educated, in music and, gulp, the black arts. Chaney's make-up is as superb as ever with its stretched nose, sunken eyes and corpse-like pallor, a commanding figure of fear.

Although lacking the avant-garde extremities and experimentation of many silent horror films, *The Phantom Of The Opera* shows that a well-crafted big budget film can hold an audience captivated, entertained and scared. Its influence is more widespread precisely because of its grounding in commercial sensibilities.

From Gold To Lead: The Thirties And Forties

For Hollywood at least, the coming of sound started a Golden Age of horror. A streak of inventive and impressive films ranging from subtle to macabre and effects-laden extravaganza took the public by storm forcing even studios unfamiliar with the genre (such as MGM) into the fray. Partly this success can be put down to two films which blazed on the screens, Tod Browning's (c.f.) *Dracula* and James Whale's (c.f.) *Frankenstein*. Both were made for Universal Pictures. Scores of imitations and similar productions were authorised and both Boris Karloff and Bela Lugosi became big enough stars to sell pictures on the strength of their names alone. Interestingly, audiences identified with the monster of the pictures rather than the bland heroes.

Following his early success, Karloff starred in an astonishing number of films. *The Mummy* (1932), an engaging tale of morbid love, saw him as the returning Egyptian Im-Ho-Tep, imprisoned for forbidden love and seeking the desecrators of his tomb. The slowly unravelling flashback structure really helps to flesh the film out and prompted sequels and remakes right up to the present day. *The Ghoul*, a British production, was even darker in tone, eschewing exotic lands for a far more grizzly form of life after death. Visually sumptuous with some extreme expressionist sets, *The Mask Of Fu Manchu* (1932) takes the pulp action and xenophobia of the popular Sax Rohmer characters and emblazons them across the screen with unbridled fetishism. Torture has never looked so sexual as the unscrupulous Fu Manchu contrives increasingly devious devices to punish the infidels, while his slinky daughter deliriously laps up every morsel of pain. Such blatant and accentuated use of sadistic violence was, however, on the way out - even non-horror films of the time would receive short shrift just a couple of years later for their frank depictions of sex and violence. Its zenith came with the stupendously violent but strangely moving classic *King Kong*, still the ultimate monster movie. *The Most Dangerous Game* (aka *The Hounds Of Zaroff*, 1932) starred the silver screen's favourite scream queen Fay Wray. The premise is so wonderfully simple it has been used in countless remakes - a mad hunter seeks the ultimate prey, man himself. Another oft-remade film started life as a vehicle for Peter Lorre; *Mad Love* (1935) features a pianist who fears that his transplanted hands have a lethal intent of their own, because they once belonged to an executed murderer. Lorre returned to the moving hand theme in *The Beast With Five Fingers* (1947).

After the Hays Code got into full swing matters became more implied (*Dracula's Daughter*'s delicately underplayed lesbianism), fantastical

18

(*Bride Of Frankenstein*'s little people also crop up in *Dr Cyclops*), rational or comedic. But an even darker cloud was on the horizon - war. World War 2 changed the tone of films considerably, away from grim Gothic horrors and into lighter, fantastical realms. Prestige productions vanished and films became more rushed, more simplistic and far less interesting. Despite a good enough start the popular comedy duo Abbot and Costello produced an increasingly irritating range of horror comedies, blunting the edge of Universal's successes with escalating juvenilia and a tendency towards slapstick. Thus Abbot and Costello met Frankenstein, the Mummy, the (long-winded) Killer Boris Karloff, the Invisible Man and Dr Jekyll And Mr Hyde - bleeding any horror and most humour dry. It was down to the smaller studios to salvage the sorry situation. RKO hired Val Lewton (c.f.) to produce a series of low-budget horror films which managed to stay (usually) within the letter of the Hays code whilst being scary and intellectually stimulating. They also made money!

Once the War was over the studios still had a few barren years ahead and the horror film was the first to feel the pinch. In the face of the cinema's biggest threat, television, the studios floundered and began to fragment. Smaller companies came into the fray and these were not worried about upsetting the status quo. More films were made in black and white again, offering far more sensationalist material than could be watched at home. Meanwhile the big names turned to epics and widescreen Technicolor to win back a dwindling audience.

King Kong (1933)

Dir: Merian Cooper & Ernest Schoedsack St: Fay Wray, Robert Armstrong

Carl Denham makes sensationalist jungle pictures and boy does he have a prime concept for his next one. Taking 'love interest' Anne to Skull Island, his leading male is none other than Kong - god to some, big scary monkey-thing to others. But his motives turn out to be even more devious as he prepares to show the "eighth wonder of the world" to a rapturous New York audience, a plan Kong is none too chuffed about.

From exotic tribal rituals to huge battling dinosaurs with multiple violent deaths and a massive primal beast ripping a bloody swathe through a major city, *King Kong* has got the lot. Willis O'Brien's exemplary special effects provided an inspiration to masses of cineastes, from future stop-frame guru Ray Harryhausen to a youthful Steven Spielberg. Its power has hardly diminished in the seventy years since its execution because of one thing - character. Kong never ceases to be a living entity, constantly swaying, scratching or responding inquisitively. He is the purest screen manifestation of the male id. He hates with gusto, he loves and protects with gusto, proving his worth to his 'mate', Anne, by wringing the life out of the island dinosaurs with his bare hands. These sequences (O'Brien also did the remarkable work on the superior 1927 version of Conan Doyle's *The Lost World*) show that the character traits are not lavished on Kong alone. Also key to the film's continued success are the characters created by Edgar Wallace's script, who are well-rounded and convincing. Fay Wray's Anne is not just the scream queen that her reputation suggests (if you faced a multi-storey killing machine of primitive aggression wouldn't you scream?) but a gutsy, adventurous lass who is very capable of standing up for herself, unless about to be sacrificed to a lumbering megabeast. By the film's close she has come to respect and even pity her captor, torn away from his natural environment to amuse the thoughtless masses. When Kong shrugs off his shackles and stampedes through the city, you cheer for him, because by this time you have come to know him.

Other, inferior, Kong films were made including a memorable one-on-one with Godzilla (Kong won in Western prints, Godzilla in Eastern) and a truly atrocious De Laurentiis produced remake in 1976. O'Brien revisited animated apes with the smaller scale weep-along *Mighty Joe Young* (1949).

The Ghoul (1933)

Dir: T Hayes Hunter St: Boris Karloff, Cedric Hardwicke, Ernest Thesiger

Professor Morlant, Egyptologist or grave robber? He has in his possession the Eternal Light, a precious jewel that will grant him immortality if the rituals performed after his death are correct. And die he does, watched by his faithful God-fearing butler Laing and the decidedly dodgy solicitor Broughton. With bickering cousins Betty and Ralph trying to get to the bottom of things, Aga Ben Dragore and Mahmoud after the jewel, Kaney falling for the silver-tongued sheikh and a replacement vicar, things can only get more complicated as the moon's rays illuminate the professor's tomb and his corpse stirs at the prospect of rebirth.

Carter's discovery of Tutankhamun's tomb made the creation of Egyptian-themed horror films an inevitability. American Universal gave us *The Mummy* (also with Karloff) while the British Gaumont furnished us with *The Ghoul*. Despite basic similarities (Egyptian theme, dead guy comes back and kills) the focus of the two is markedly different - *The Mummy* plays the macabre love aspect by having an ages old corpse manipulated beyond his control, while *The Ghoul* has a man obsessed with his own mortality trying to cheat death. *The Ghoul* is a morbid and dark affair, Morlant insisting that the jewel is bandaged into his hand so that when he dies it remains with him. That it is stolen and hidden in a jar of coffee straight after incarceration shows the futility of his actions. He is so ingrained in the cultural trappings of an ancient mythology he risks his fortune on a macabre dream, even taking on the looks of a mummified corpse before he is dead. When he awakens enraged at the loss of the jewel (and the limited time he therefore has to affirm his immortality) he becomes almost superhuman in power - he is defined entirely by his selfish desires. The other characters are far more complex, particularly in the case of Laing, Broughton and Nigel Hartley (the sinister parson) all of whom have varying motivations that unravel as the film progresses. After such a grim opening, the addition of Kaney, Betty's dotty friend, is essential to lighten the tone, which up until then is thicker than the London smog that dominates the city scenes.

Dead Of Night (1945)

Dir: Alberto Cavalcanti, Charles Crichton, Basil Dearden, Robert Hammer

Walter Craig is unprepared for meeting a group of people that he recognises but has never met. They are part of his recurring nightmare and he fears for the worst. As they relay increasingly strange supernatural tales, it becomes clear that Walter's nightly visions are demonstrative of actual occurrences. So how do they stop the inevitable spiral into murder and madness?

The horror anthology film is a staple favourite, popularised by Milton Subotsky films like *Dr Terror's House Of Horrors* and *Vault Of Horror* right through to *Creepshow I & II* and *Cat's Eye*. The format remains generally the same - take a linking story with a repetitive motif, tell the tales and finish it all up with a twist. It allows the opportunity to take several good tales but not let them outlive their welcome by stretching their premises. These are the cinematic equivalent of ghostly short stories, now largely taken over by short horror/shock television shows like *Tales Of The Unexpected* or *Tales From The Crypt*. *Dead Of Night* is an early example of the subgenre and without doubt hugely influential. It is one of the few examples of decent British horror in the Forties. The five tales, based on works by among others Angus MacPhail (who also helped pen the screenplay) and HG Wells, are of varying length, accommodating the screen time for as long as necessary. There's the racing driver who avoids being killed in a bus crash following a premonition featuring the bus conductor as an undertaker, Sally's "subconscious thingamajig" where she comforts a murdered child, and the tale of Potter and Parrot, two golfers who play a round for the hand of a girl, only to have the loser (Parrot cheated) commit suicide and return as an irritated ghost. The story of Peter seeing the reflections of a different room in a mirror is both creepy and surreal, he slowly loses his mind and adopts the persona of the mirror's original owner. This macabre tale was repeated in the Amicus omnibus film *From Beyond The Grave* (1973) to lesser effect. The final tale stars Michael Redgrave as a ventriloquist and is concerned with the takeover of personality. It also inspired a remake in the shape of Richard Attenborough's preposterous and overlong *Magic* (1979). Blessed with some imaginative lighting and a drop dead ending that is brilliantly executed (all Dutch tilts and surreal claustrophobic juxtapositions) *Dead Of Night* remains a fascinating experiment from Ealing Studios.

You'd Be Paranoid If You Knew You Were Next: The Fifties

The Fifties saw America become a dominant force in world affairs. After World War Two, a boom generation of affluent devil-may-care teenagers burst on the scene, upsetting their parents' values and driving their motor cars. This created the two primary themes in Fifties American horror cinema – the teen drive-in flick and the McCarthyist paranoia film. Following on from the high-profile trials against Communism that formed the basis of the House Unamerican Activities Committee it was natural that film-makers should turn to the fear of Communism as a theme for their films. The dread of alien threat can be seen in Robert Wise's thoughtful plea for peace – *The Day The Earth Stood Still* (1951) where human ignorance and intolerance of the alien almost causes the Earth's downfall. In sharp contrast *Earth Vs The Flying Saucers* (1956) sees the other as oppressive faceless horde - the alien/Communist conspiracy to be fought with patriotic verve by All-American men. Essentially fear of science and fear of Communism are two sides of the same coin, representing the unknown and being taken over by something beyond your control. To this end, many horror themes approached science fiction but in reality just mirrored the fears of their time. This was not limited to the USA – Japan gave us *Godzilla* (*Gojira*) which blamed America's nuclear testing on the destruction of society.

The American teenager market had an insatiable appetite for trashy films. This was the birth of the drive-in generation. The exploitation films provided the requisite hotchpotch of dreamy teen idols, frugging chicks and gung-ho horror. Add a little rock 'n' roll to the piece and, voilà, bums in Chevys. *How To Make A Monster* (1958) and *I Was A Teenage Werewolf* (1957) are typical examples of knowingly kitsch exploitation fodder. Companies came and companies went, but one maintained a longevity that many major studios would envy: American International Pictures. AIP's success lay in giving its undiscerning public exactly what they wanted, but it also provided a rich pool of talent for the next generation of film-makers. Its chief proponent was Roger Corman, who wrote, produced and directed more pictures than he'd probably care to remember including *It Conquered The World* (1956), featuring a giant killer cucumber and the cheesy *Attack Of The Crab Monsters* (1957). Alongside Corman in the low-budget field, director and producer William Castle was astonishing audiences with his own unique brand of high concept exploitation and outrageous use of gimmicks. Films such as *The Tingler* (1959), where the cinema seats were wired up to produce a mild electric shock, and *The House On Haunted Hill* (1958), which featured an Emergo inflatable skeleton appearing from the screen, are remembered as much for their campaigns as the finished products, which also offer much to enjoy.

In England, Hammer Studios adapted Nigel Kneale's hugely successful BBC television series *The Quatermass Experiment* for the big screen. The international success of the film led the company to invest in colour film stock for the first of their Gothic horror films, *The Curse Of Frankenstein*. It made stars of long time actors Peter Cushing and Christopher Lee. The pair were reunited in many of Hammer's subsequent productions, including Terence Fisher's (c.f.) awesome *The Horror Of Dracula*. Hammer would become Britain's most prominent horror producer in the Sixties.

The Quatermass Experiment (1955)

Dir: Val Guest St: Brian Donlevy

"I launched 'em and I bought 'em back," announces Professor Quatermass glibly, failing to mention that his rocket came back to the wrong place, ignited half the countryside and has left two of the three astronauts jellybabies. Worse, the survivor Victor is rapidly turning into a life-draining alien with a cactus for an arm.

Nigel Kneale's television series had gripped a nation and provided Hammer with an ideal vehicle for a cinema outing, giving them the opportunity to show what television couldn't, especially as much of the original programmes were broadcast live. The transition from small to big screen was as much a burden as a benefit, the extended budget allowed Guest the luxury of some impressive effects and backdrops - the crashed rocket is a very powerful image of failed science while the final sequences in Westminster Abbey are convincingly realised. Even better is the make-up work which renders Victor a translucent, sick man undergoing a strange metamorphosis while the bodies of his unfortunate victims are hideously disfigured, drained of all life. It is no surprise that the horrific element of the film was played up. Guest playfully keeps the camera on the move, constantly tracking onto objects or people to enhance the sense of urgency and is not afraid to rely on audience genre knowledge to increase tension. Victor meeting the little girl mirrors *Frankenstein* (another unwitting monster created by science gone wrong and also titled through its creator not its creation) so that we assume that the child is going to die. But Guest fools us and in doing so shows that there is a spark of humanity left in Victor, his subsequent appearance as 'all vegetable' provoking a sympathetic reaction.

The Quatermass Experiment suffers from two major flaws that deadens its impact; the script has been cut down considerably, reducing the more philosophical arguments of the original and then there is Prof Quatermass himself. In an attempt to bolster international returns from the film it was decided to cast Brian Donlevy in the title role, which was a big mistake. Instead of a reasoned scientist wracked with guilt but compelled to push the frontiers of human knowledge, we are given a loud, brash, thug of a man without a single sympathetic characteristic. His transference of guilt to anyone in sight is truly remarkable. Still there is enough of Kneale's original to make the film a classic and Guest's direction makes the whole affair eminently watchable. Two further Hammer Quatermass films were made, *Quatermass II* (1957) and the superior *Quatermass And The Pit* (1967) and Nigel Kneale would go on to script *The Abominable Snowman* (1957).

Invasion Of The Body Snatchers (1956)

Dir: Don Siegel St: Dana Wynter, Kevin McCarthy

Miles is having a tough time getting through to people - they're all veg-etables. Literally. Cultivated from alien pods in greenhouses like giant peas, only human, these leggy legumes are replacing their meaty counter-parts while they sleep, assimilating their looks but not their feelings. It's all Miles can do to try and make the authorities believe him but, eventually, everyone needs to sleep...

"At first glance everything looked the same, it wasn't. Something evil had taken over the town." Siegel's paranoid nightmare is a perfect example of lean scripting and tight narrative focus, the apparent normality of it all being the most horrific thing. The film has been seen by some as a vindica-tion of the McCarthy witch-hunts of the Fifties, the perils of allowing your neighbourhood to be overtaken by communists. On the other hand it can be viewed as being for the rights of the individual to stand up against govern-mental restrictions on its citizens' freedoms. Regardless, the paranoia is convincing, the prospect of "no pain ...born into another world...where everyone's the same" may bring comfort and support, but removes free will and the ability to make mistakes as well as triumph. Siegel tightly composes his images to show the world slowly closing in on Miles, filming the mundane with a slight air of unreality, the truth dawning gradually on both Miles and the viewer. The very blandness of the framing early on means that when we are finally shown the pods in the greenhouse, the extreme Dutch tilt makes the experience more horrific by its abuse of the screen language used till that point. The pods themselves are wonderfully sticky and their humanoid offspring chillingly devoid of identity until they have assimilated their victims. It is the speed with which they replace their human doubles that provides the film with its shocks and increases the paranoia to feverish levels.

Although themes from *Invasion Of The Body Snatchers* crop up time and again, two direct remakes have sought to relate the film to their time. Philip Kaufman's 1978 version expands the running time, budget and aspect ratio of the original to good effect although it remains less focused, while Abel Ferrara's overhaul unnecessarily places it in a military context but is surprisingly watchable (and, for Ferrara, uncontroversial!)

Les Yeux Sans Visage (Eyes Without A Face) (1959)

Dir: Georges Franju St: Pierre Brasseur, Alida Valli, Edith Scob

Respected authority on skin grafting Professor Génessier needs to rebuild the face of his daughter Christiane, mutilated in a car crash because of his demonic driving. Assisted by Louise, a former patient, he uses kidnapped girls as face donors. Hidden behind an expressionless mask, the world thinks her dead and for the most part, Christiane wishes she was.

Les Yeux Sans Visage marks the thin boundary between pulp and art. Combining the lurid excesses of the fantastique with a painterly eye for Sadean beauty, the film leaves an indelible mark on anyone who sees it. Despite being over forty years old and filmed in black and white, its capacity to shock has hardly diminished - the scene of the Professor's attempts at grafting the face of a kidnapped girl onto his daughter is both surprisingly graphic and takes an excruciating length of time. Being a melodrama the sacrifices for Christiane's face are in vain, we are shown her tearful deterioration in a series of clinical photographs that chart her progress from beautiful to irrefutably decomposed. Yet despite its sordid nature, this remains at heart a symbolic art film with Cocteau-style dreamlike wanderings and beauty in the face of horror. The prevailing image is of Christiane wandering in her mask a lonely figure, phoning her fiancé without speaking and, finally, walking out in the sunshine, free as the doves that flutter around her.

Louise commits atrocious acts for the Professor because he reconstructed her face but she is no more important than the hounds that he keeps for experimentation - her dog collar of pearls hiding her scar tissue emphasises her status. Christiane too is a pitiful figure. Disfigured to the point that only her eyes remain, she wears an emotionless mask. Denied access to a mirror she can still see herself in windows or, frighteningly, the blade of a knife. She doesn't want to live but has no choice in her destiny, officially dead and at the mercy of her father. From the opening shot of a raincoated woman dumping a naked body to the final shot of uncertainty as Christiane stumbles into the beauty of the day, *Les Yeux Sans Visage* is a near faultless combination of high art and popularist exploitation.

The film's influence on Jesus Franco's *Dr Orloff* films is marked but there are also resonances in works as diverse as Tony Scott's *The Hunger* (1983), John Woo's *Face/Off* (1997) and the works of Cronenberg (c.f.) and Argento (c.f.). Franju's most celebrated film fits neatly into that small (but wonderful) body of French pulp melodrama that stretches from Feuillade to Jean Rollin.

Psychos And Swingers: The Sixties

The Sixties' reputation as an era of permissiveness was ushered in with two films that were critically derided as offensive and macabre. Hitchcock's *Psycho* (1960) became a huge commercial success but the superior *Peeping Tom* effectively ended the career of its creator Michael Powell. *Psycho*'s strength lay in its intent to simply scare the audience. That we are ultimately given a justification for Norman Bates' barbaric actions does little to diminish their effect. The impact of *Psycho* was immediate, the twisted murderer film became a popular entry in early Sixties cinema. Its more downmarket offspring can be seen in the stalk and slash films of the late Seventies and early Eighties. Hitchcock's next film *The Birds* (1963) also proved to be inspirational in its depiction of nature gone mad. No explanation is given for the birds' attack and no solution is found by the film's close. It remains one of the most resolutely nihilistic of mainstream cinema. Psychological horror developed as a form that could be placed in the real world and therefore did not alienate mainstream audiences with specific genre ideas. Roman Polanski's *Repulsion* (1965) dealt with a young woman's descent into sexual madness and *Whatever Happened To Baby Jane?* (1962) featured remarkable performances from Joan Crawford and Bette Davis as a pair of feuding sisters.

Roger Corman continued his stranglehold on the low-budget market but was improving the quality of some of his more prestigious productions. While *Little Shop Of Horrors* (1960) is unashamedly cheap, it nonetheless benefits from witty scripting and an enthusiastic cast (including Jack Nicholson as a masochistic dental patient) but it was with *Fall Of The House Of Usher* (1960) that Corman made an intelligent horror film on a small budget using full colour. This marked the beginning of his cycle of films based on the works of Edgar Allen Poe including the *Pit And The Pendulum* (1961), the witty portmanteau *Tales Of Terror* (1962) with sterling performances from Peter Lorre and Basil Rathbone opposite Vincent Price, and the more serious *Tomb Of Ligeia* (1964) and *The Haunted Palace* (1963). The horrific closing of *X - The Man With X-Ray Eyes* (1963), where Ray Milland plucks out his own eyes to stop his tormented visions still has the power to chill, despite the essentially trashy concept.

Corman and his protégés represented the posh end of the low-budget market. Other independent producers were not so discerning when it came to taste, talent or imagination. Most renowned is perhaps Herschell Gordon Lewis, a no-budget film-maker who introduced hard-core gore to unsuspecting and undemanding drive-ins when the bottom had dropped out of the nudie market. *Blood Feast* (1963) features such delights as splattered brains, naked bathing models having their legs amputated and, most notoriously, a woman having her tongue wrenched from her mouth. His later films continued to pile on the atrocities (*Two Thousand Maniacs* (1964), *The Gruesome Twosome* (1967), *The Wizard Of Gore* (1970)) but their inept handling render their excesses laughable rather than upsetting.

In England, Hammer were at the height of their technical and artistic powers. This really was their golden era tackling everything from class exploitation in John Gilling's astonishing 1966 *The Plague Of The Zombies* (a Cornish mine owner uses zombies as free labour, this film features some remarkable dream imagery of corpse hands bursting from beyond the grave) to the ritualistic aspects of black magic in Terence Fisher's *The Devil Rides Out*. The company couldn't put a foot wrong. Further sequels of popular Hammer films, particularly from the vampire (*Kiss Of The Vampire*, *Brides Of Dracula*) and Frankenstein series continued to thrill audiences. Hammer became glossier, gorier, more colourful and more camp. However, by the close of the decade the company was clearly in decline. Hammer's death throes were long and occasionally embarrassing. Their plot foundations in literature left them out of touch with a society brought up on graphic images of the Vietnam war. They could not hope to compete with the nastiness of US films or the sexuality of European ones.

Perhaps one of the greatest losses to British horror cinema was that of Michael Reeves who had begun his trade in Italy, working on *Castle Of The Living Dead* (1964) and *Revenge Of The Blood Beast* (1965) starring Barbara Steele before returning to England. With Tigon Films he produced *The Sorcerers* (1967), a grim and hallucinogenic tale of psychic links. His final film *Witchfinder General* (1968) is one of the least compromising of British films, a murky depiction of state-sanctioned torture and a hero who, by the film's close, has lost his woman and his mind. Sadly Reeves died in 1969 aged 25. Europe had taken Hammer's period gloss and transformed it into a colourful combination of art and kitsch. Leading the field were Italian directors such as Riccardo Freda and Mario Bava who were creating the kind of sexy yet violent shockers that Hammer could only dream of and Americans could only ban.

The swinging Sixties certainly showed a change in audience attitudes as to what they were permitted to see and what they wanted to challenge. Very much a transitional period - people were developing and maturing away from Fifties' ideologies - the genre was attracting increasing numbers of film-makers. However it was a small black and white film made in Pittsburgh for a pittance that ushered a new era of graphic violence. That film was *Night Of The Living Dead* (1968), its director was George A Romero (c.f.) and its success meant that even the big studios had to sit up and take horror seriously once more.

Peeping Tom (1960)

Dir: Michael Powell St: Carl Boehm, Moira Shearer, Anna Massey

Mark Lewis would kill to see a good movie. Actually he does, stalking buxom prostitutes and 'artists' models' with his portable camera, he films them while they die. He is such a confused boy you see, and very shy too. He needs a nice girlfriend to take him from this madness of death and celluloid, which is where lodger Helen comes in.

Peeping Tom wasn't so much derided on release, it was witch-hunted. No one could understand how Michael Powell, one of the most idiosyncratic but respected of British directors (normally working with Emeric Pressberger) could have produced such a sleazy work. Cut by the censors, mutilated by the critics it virtually ruined his distinguished career. Now it is praised as a classic and often compared to Hitchcock's *Psycho*. Despite some similarities though, the films are poles apart; *Peeping Tom* derives its psychosis from the father, is in glorious saturated colour, is more British than the Queen and has characters that you actually care for. If Hitchcock's film is an exercise in manipulating audiences through the language of cinema then Powell's is about cinema full stop. Despite its immersion in British underculture (the kind we don't tell outsiders about, like newsagent-distributed pornography) Powell resolutely avoids realism in the quest for a vision of voyeurism that is purely cinematic. In the opening sequence we follow a prostitute to her death from the point of view of the perpetrator implicating the viewer in the act, but drawing attention to the fact that we are looking through a camera's viewfinder. In one shot we are perpetrator and audience, helpless to prevent a crime that has already happened. The rest of the film is similarly strewn with images of cinema but the most disturbing sequence is reserved for the films that Mark's father took of him as a child. Treating the boy as a guinea pig we watch dumbstruck as he is terrified in the name of science (chillingly the father is Powell himself). If we didn't have sympathies for him previously, we do now. Unlike Norman Bates, who seems a snivelling mummy's boy, Mark is the result of an inhuman life at the hands of his father. His camera ties him to his past, a surrogate child for him to protect and feed with images of pain and suffering. The relationship between Helen and Mark is moving because of its ultimate futility - his crimes are so horrendous that there can be no redemption for him. When Helen finds out the awful extent of his killings, the manner in which he subjects his victims to an endless loop of their own lives drain-ing before them, the circle is complete. If cinema kills the viewer it can also kill the maker. Powerful, chilling and beautifully shot, *Peeping Tom* has at last regained its rightful place as a masterpiece of British cinema.

The Masque Of The Red Death (1964)

Dir & Prd: Roger Corman St: Vincent Price, Jane Asher, Hazel Court

Prosperous Prince Prospero considers the villagers rabble, even though they provide his opulent trappings and desirable residence by their misera-ble labour. He burns the village, tries to get pretty Francesca to bed him and imprisons her father and boyfriend just to get a bit of leverage in the nuptial department. Still, he was probably doing them a favour because the excruciatingly painful red death is abroad, so view the incineration as a precautionary cauterising. With all that grimness going on Prospero needs a jolly good masque to cheer himself up. But with any decent bash there are always gatecrashers...

While all Corman's Poe films are triumphs of film-making over budget, *The Masque Of The Red Death* marks the cycle's finest hour and is a per-fect realisation of Corman's basic rule of exploitation cinema - give the audience regular hints of nudity and/or violence. Aligned to this is the prin-ciple that you put as much on the screen as your limitations will allow. Thus *The Masque Of The Red Death* is in cinescope and full colour and looks far more expansive and expensive than it actually is. Cinematogra-pher and future director Nicholas Roeg saturates the screen with a chro-matic intensity - electric blue mists with crimson cloaked harbinger monk, brightly lit sunflower yellow rooms or a white rose engorged with deep red blood. Price's Prospero is unremittingly cruel, viewing peasants as enter-tainment and even his guests as disposable playthings. He is open in his worship of Satan - the masquerade provides further fuel for his ritualistic excesses. The two most interesting characters are Juliana and Francesca, the former and future companions of Prospero. Their relationship adds depth to the film - Juliana has been usurped but ultimately Francesca just wants to escape with her men. By the end though, her complicity in Pros-pero's atrocities ensure that the evil around her has changed her outlook, she has become aloof because of his ceaseless striving for destruction. Juli-ana has realised the error of her decadent lifestyle, "I am betrothed to the Devil" but it is too late - her long-time devotion is rewarded by being sav-aged by a huge bird amidst the loud ticking of an axe-pendulumed clock. Corman manages to imbue the film with a Grimm air of fairy-tale decrepi-tude mixed with Crowleyesque ethos of "do what thou wilt." Add a rhythmic sacrificial dream sequence and a rainbow-coloured pretentious ending where angels of death meet up after a tough day at the office, and the result is a combination of knowing artiness and Grand-Guignol exploitative horror that makes it a classic. Not as subtle as *Tombs Of Ligeia* or as camp as *The Raven* but a prime example of the Corman ethos at its finest.

Rosemary's Baby (1968)

Dir: Roman Polanski St: Mia Farrow, John Cassavetes

"Let's have a baby." Rosemary and Guy's approach to procreation starts with a bang once they move into The Bramford, a sumptuous apartment block. Guy's an actor whose luck is coincidentally improving since neighbours Minnie and Roman Castavet made themselves part of the household. But as Rosemary's happy day approaches, can she be sure that her oven bun isn't going to be appropriated for nefarious necromantic purposes and, with strange chanting, grotesque dreams and dubious herby milkshakes to contend with, who can she trust?

Rosemary's Baby may well be nit-pickingly accurate to Ira Levin's novel but remains resolutely Polanski's film. Taking the elements of abnormal niceness hiding a dark undercurrent, Polanski manages to weave elements of the surreal and psychological that epitomise his best work. Like *Repulsion*, we witness the slow psychological decline of the central character and empathise with her by sharing her dreams and hallucinations. Rosemary's dreams invade her 'real' space - her rape by the devil is shown in a half-drugged state to the loud clicking of their clock as she is ritually marked with symbols by her naked neighbours. It becomes more disturbing when, upon awakening, her husband pretends it was he who molested her - "It was kinda fun in a necrophile way." The Castavets, especially the permanently grinning Minnie, are deeply disturbing individuals yet remain believable as 'innocents' because of their age and amiability. The sleight of hand from what we suspect (bad) and what is actually going on (also bad) is classic misdirection but the final acceptance of Rosemary's role in the proceedings makes the film genuinely chilling.

Even now, the elements that make *Rosemary's Baby* so disturbing have not diminished - the fear of violation, psychological delusions and paranoia that your friends are your enemies - and yet it remains very much a product of its time. Polanski's distinct and unsettling use of low, long, static shots followed by intimate but deranged handheld work constantly keeps you on the edge. Even though its infamy has paled after the huge success of *The Exorcist* it remains a far more cerebral, mature and unsettling work that plays subtlety over shock tactics... except when necessary.

The Decade That Taste Forgot: The Seventies

The Seventies may have been an affront to taste when it came to fashion, but that tastelessness also extended to the films of the period. Flower power had gone sour and the boundaries of censorship were being broken throughout America and Europe (Britain, however, clung on regardless). Especially for America, the tone of its films took a turn to the darker side and for once the studios were listening as well. Film production diversified. The big players produced more confrontational, glossy and expensive horror films to compete with the plethora of independents who, in turn, responded with even more visceral and challenging material. Approaches to horror lay in effects realisation and production technology, which had increased in leaps and bounds. Innovation such as this hadn't really been seen since the Universal pictures of the Thirties. *The Exorcist*'s pioneering use of effects work and prosthetics launched the cult of the make-up man as intrinsic to the final product. Rick Baker, Tom Savini and Stan Winston would become stars in their own rights for creating the gruesome monsters and the consequent carnage resulting from their actions.

Hollywood followed the success of *The Exorcist* (c.f.) with other demonically based projects. *The Omen* (1976) is a portentous and overblown production about Robert Thorn (Gregory Peck) slowly realising that the son he has raised is not his, but the Devil's. It works because it takes its ludicrous premise seriously. It is also notable for its convoluted death sequences that would plague horror films to the present day, including an impaled priest, a suicidal nanny and a preposterous decapitation with a pane of glass. It proved successful enough to spawn three sequels.

Environmental concerns were finding a voice in the most unlikely of productions. Steven Spielberg's snack-on-a-bather-fest *Jaws* (1975), is still the most revolting PG-rated film ever passed. Irwin Allen, producer of many an overblown and overlong disaster movie (*Earthquake*, *The Towering Inferno*) gave us the hysterical killer bee film *The Swarm*. Progressively downmarket audiences were treated to such delights as *Squirm* (electrically raised mutant worms), *Night Of The Lepus* (killer rabbits), *Frogs* (tagline 'Don't go near the pond'), *Phase IV* (ants), *Empire Of The Ants* (giant ants, this time ineptly beaten with a broomstick by Joan Collins), *The Giant Spider Invasion* with a hairy spider covered van as the main villain, and the killer rat films *Willard* and *Ben*.

Many of today's most highly regarded and established horror directors had their roots firmly planted in the Seventies. Both Wes Craven's *Last House On The Left* and Tobe Hooper's *The Texas Chainsaw Massacre* were considered unacceptable viewing for British audiences and effectively banned. Hooper went on to make the backwater alligator and scythe horror comedy *Death Trap* (1977), the creepy vampire TV series *Salem's Lot* (1979), and the overrated and anaemic *Poltergeist* (1982) before continuing his career in an amiable but ultimately lacklustre shadow of his former glories. Others who found themselves carving out their careers included Joe Dante (c.f.), Brian De Palma, Canada's David Cronenberg (c.f.) and John Carpenter. Carpenter's *Halloween* (1978) was unusual in that most of the murders, while surreal, were not excessively graphic. Carpenter replaced the viscera of his contemporaries with tension, suspense and silky smooth steadicam. The figure of 'The Shape,' convicted lunatic Michael Myers, gives the film an urban mythic atmosphere that is emphasised by its holiday title. Set entirely on one night, it laid the ground rules for virtually every stalk and slash film that was made in its wake. Carpenter turned to the campfire horror *The Fog* (1979) and consolidated his 'modern master of the suspense' status with a string of horror and science fiction hits in the Eighties and Nineties.

As Hollywood was producing gloss, the ultra low market was producing dross, proving that the spirit of Herschell Gordon Lewis was not gone. Troma Films trail-blazed their unashamedly tasteless no-brainer horror films to cater for a very specialised audience. A combination of cheesecake nudity and hard-core gore, Troma films wallow in their B-movie status bringing attention to their very cheapness. Their first film was the irresponsible, puerile and unacceptable *Blood Sucking Freaks* (aka *The Incredible Torture Show*, 1976) featuring a demented dwarf who tortures and mutilates naked women. Featured 'highlights' include disembowelments, dismemberment, a human dartboard and one victim having her brains sucked out through a straw. Yuck. Their later films, such as *The Toxic Avenger* (1985) became more knowingly funny but often no less sick.

Not that all the terror was restricted to that side of the pond - our European cousins were also hard at work. Spain's Paul Naschy was single-handedly producing a variety of work ranging from slapstick horror comedy to the dark unpleasantries of *The Hunchback Of The Morgue* (1972). Another Spaniard, the prolific ex-pat Jesus Franco was continuing his assault on the eyes and ears of the world with an increasingly eclectic mix of sadism, torture and blatant pornography. His sheer output has meant that at least some of it is watchable, *Vampiros Lesbos* (1970) and *Succubus* (1967) being amongst his best. Italy's indefatigable ability to purloin other people's successful formulae was matched only by its tolerance of artists with grandiose operatic and sometimes just plain barmy ideas. Mario Bava continued his career with some beautifully shot, coloured and edited tales of death. *Twist Of The Death Nerve* (aka *Bay Of Blood,* 1971) predates the late Seventies slasher movement in its Agatha Christie derived succession of bizarre murders and grotesque characters. *Five Dolls For An August Moon* (1970) was in a similar vein, but he was at his best when dealing with warped internalised necrophilic sexuality - in the much misunderstood *Baron Blood* (1972) and *Lisa And The Devil* (1972). Bava's tendency to imbue his scenery with as much character as his cast finds its beginnings in his remarkable debut *The Mask Of Satan* (1960) and can be seen in his supervisory role on Dario Argento's (c.f.) *Inferno*.

In Britain, Hammer may have been fizzling out but Milton Subotsky's Amicus Productions provided a combination of period anthology horror films and misjudged funky modern-day shockers including *The Beast Must Die* (1974) and *Scream And Scream Again* (1969). Other low-budget British films came from Peter Walker who gave us the mad judge classic *House Of Whipcord* (1974) and the demented DIY tool murders of *Frightmare* (1974), while Norman J Warren produced the gratuitous *Satan's Slave* (1976), *Terror* (1978) and the tasteless *Alien* rip-off *Inseminoid* (1980).

Theater Of Blood (1972)

Dir: Douglas Hickox St: Vincent Price, Diana Rigg, Robert Morley, Eric Sykes

"It's Lionheart all right. Only he would have the temerity to rewrite Shakespeare." The members of the Critics Circle are dwindling, each gruesomely murdered in a manner reflecting the works of The Bard. Edward Lionheart's reputation was consistently sullied by the critics - snubbed during their awards ceremony he apparently committed suicide, leaving a grieving daughter. But he lives, reinventing Shakespeare's finest works for a new, captive, audience.

"It's hardly comedy sergeant." Oh we beg to differ. Outrageous comedy with lashings of gore and unexpected deaths *Theater Of Blood* repays with every subsequent viewing. Consciously camp and hammy with a cast of British comedy veterans, the often explicit proceedings are rendered hysterical because of the tone of the affair and a perfectly overblown performance from Vincent Price. Add to that Hickox's extreme use of deep focused lenses to produce distorted and out-of-proportion framings and you have an expertly weird *Avengers*-style black comedy that never flags. The script is morbidly deadpan and soaring in its convoluted excesses. Like the Dr Phibes films, *Theater Of Blood* takes a thematic approach to murder, a pulpy device that has served crime and horror writers well. Instead of the plagues of Egypt from *Dr Phibes Rises Again* or the seven deadly sins of *Se7en*, the murder 'thème du jour' is Shakespearean tragedies. It's an inspired idea that allows Price the full range of larger-than-life roles, the opportunity for some gratuitously flowery dialogue with plenty of rolling vowels and some outlandish set pieces. Maxwell is slashed to death by Lionheart's tramp troupe on the Ides of March, Snipe is grabbed, speared and dragged behind a horse along the cemetery gravel ("He was meant to be one of the mourners") and lecherous Dickman has 1lb 2ozs, sorry 1lb, of flesh removed. Arthur Lowe's Horace Sprout has his head removed in his own bedroom while his wife lies sedated beside him, in a wonderful scene where Lionheart's assistant mops his brow to some deeply inappropriate (but very funny) dramatic music. Then poor old Meredith has his 'babies' (two poodles) force-fed to him in a pie. This would be all a bit depressing were it not for the impishness of all concerned - Price as hairdresser ("dishy, dishy hair baby"), Richard III, the chef on This Is Your Dish, the saucy masseur of Diana Dors, a sinister bobby - a cornucopia of meaty roles (rolls?) stuffed with ham and aplomb. Great fun.

The Exorcist (1973)

Dir: William Friedkin St: Linda Blair, Max Von Sydow

Chris seeks medical assistance for her daughter Regan, whose behavioural problems are becoming intolerable. However, the psychiatrist she initially consults has an unusual solution. She should call in an Exorcist to rid Regan of her demonic curse.

Constantly ranked as one of the most watched of all horror films, *The Exorcist* is the stuff of legends. Hyped to the max on its release, reports of curses, mysterious accidents and related deaths enhanced the reputation of the film before anyone had even seen it. Of course audiences flocked and fainted in droves - they were so wound up by the long queues and the anticipation it was inevitable. Ostensibly the main sources of *The Exorcist*'s power remain the dogmatic belief in evil and the fact that the victim of a motiveless possession is a normal girl. The addition of Rick Baker's outstanding make-up work and some truly believable special effects makes it all the more unnerving. Whether levitating in her bed, invoking telekinetic wrath, or spewing a stream of pea-green vomit, the shocks are relentless and unnerving. The soundtrack, with backtracked animal groans, adds a further shiver-inducing feeling and all this is rounded off by low-key photography that gives the film, at times, an almost documentary quality. It fails, however, in the editing. Friedkin builds up a scene to feverish hysteria and then cuts abruptly mid-atrocity, which brings the viewer crashing to earth, diminishing the overall intention. Also Regan's possession seems to be the least of her worries compared with the graphic experiments to which she is subjected by parapsychologists. Still, it does retain a lot of its power to shock, something that in all honesty can't be claimed of the sequel, *Exorcist II: The Heretic*. Writer Blatty himself directed *Exorcist III* which, while unsettling, bears little direct reference to the first two.

The Texas Chainsaw Massacre (1974)

Dir: Tobe Hooper St: Marilyn Burns, Gunnar Hansen

Any similarities to the Scooby Doo gang are purely coincidental as a group of bickering teens drive their own Mystery Machine into the heart of Texas and the heart of darkness. Terrifying and true...

The Texas Chainsaw Massacre is one of the most notorious films ever, with a fearsome reputation that ensured both its success and consequent banning in the UK. The whole film plays on creating a myth for itself. The title alone gives the game away, but also claims that the film was based on a true story (it wasn't, it was very loosely connected to the Ed Gein killings, but then so were *Psycho* and *Deranged*) affecting audience expectations before it has even started. The key to the tension is the excruciating pacing once things get going. There is no stopping for breath at any point. It is a relentless and disturbing roller-coaster ride - the chase scenes are loud and frenzied, the quiet moments have an eerie atmosphere you can cut with a knife. This is quite simply totally assured and thoroughly manipulative film-making. If examined closely there is very little blood - the horror lies in what the audience believe they saw, and that is far more powerful. What makes it work is that it is completely over the top, everything is done to excess. When the family capture Sally, and let grandfather have a bash at torturing her, the scene is excruciating - egged on by everyone, he keeps missing, extending her ordeal. It's not without its moments of humour too, although you'll probably only spot them second time around. When Sally finally makes it to safety, only to be recaptured again, she's bundled up and shoved into a van, but her perpetrator realises he's left the lights on in the shack and has to return to switch them off. The set design is superb, particularly the family's house, with the macabre furniture made from bones and feathers, and the tin door behind which Leatherface lurks. If Hooper never entirely lived up to expectations in his later films he only has himself to blame - *The Texas Chainsaw Massacre* is an audacious debut by anyone's standards.

Suppression And Repetition: The Eighties

If the Seventies produced an uncontrollable gleeful free-for-all of sadism and excess, the Eighties would see that kind of freedom mercilessly suppressed. Starting the decade it was business as usual - William Lustig provided us with the unbearably tense and occasionally unwatchably graphic *Maniac* (1980) prompting a slew of criticism especially regarding the treatment of women. Other stalk and slash films were likewise suffering from a combination of critical outrage and lacklustre box-office returns. Even in mainstream movies such as *An American Werewolf In London* (1981), the level and intensity of gore was substantial, certainly for a film that was ostensibly a comedy. Landis' finest hour was the product of artistic freedom.

Lucio Fulchi took the opportunity (as did many Italian directors) to jump on the 'living dead' bandwagon, following the success of Romero's *Dawn Of The Dead* (c.f.). *Zombie Flesh Eaters* (1979) is sporadically beautifully shot, but emphasises the nasty side of Romero's work, as opposed to the political one. While the oft-cut shot of a woman slowly having her eye impaled on a pointed stick has been restored, many other scenes of cannibalism and mutilation are usually cut. Fulchi continued in this visceral vein with *House By The Cemetery* (1981), *City Of The Living Dead* (1980) and *The Beyond* (1981), a surreal, convoluted and impenetrable but engaging mash of every conceivable splatter idea.

Undoubtedly there were some very unpleasant films made during this time (*Cannibal Ferox* (Lenzi, 1981) etc.) so inevitably the unfettered freedom and gruesome special effects were not to last. By the opening of the decade the video cassette recorder had come down in price significantly so videotapes for hire meant that these predominantly cinema-based films were now available to view in the home. A smear campaign was orchestrated against the so-called video nasties, which resulted in heavy cutting and even banning of many horror films, following the 1984 Video Recordings Act. Additionally, America was undergoing changes to its rating system which meant many films would become more restricted. As such, on both sides of the Atlantic, film-makers were asked to compromise their vision, to make adult films suitable for a family audience.

Tightening censorship didn't necessarily mean that there was less violence or gore on the screens - it reduced the extension of pain and the dwelling on the act of aggression. Along with the outmoded and misogynist attitudes of the slasher flick, grimy film stock was also on the way out - films as unpleasant as their predecessors suddenly looked, well, cleaner and even wholesome. Film-makers sanitised their product or turned to comedy. Lamentably, horror's role model became the quintessential frat-flick *Porky's* (1981) and proceeded to parade a sorry bunch of vacuous teens through soft-core fumblings, icky prosthetics and conservative morality. *Fright Night* (1985) remains one of the better of these - at least it has the conviction to be scary, violent and have, heaven forbid, a subtext amidst the atrocious make-up (on the actors that is, the vampires are fine!). *Vamp* (1986), featuring a stripping Grace Jones vampire, starts with enough seedy promise but swiftly goes the way of repentance and remorse that so often typifies the genre – "I dallied with Evil, my friends are dead and now I see how stupid I really was."

Floundering, desperate producers set about recycling films and the Eighties became the era of the horror franchise. Sequels and related films were nothing new (*Dracula, James Bond*) but never before with such a cohesive pattern of numbering. If *The Omen* had started it all, then lower budget films would take it to its logical conclusion. John Carpenter's elegant, scary parable *Halloween* produced a sequel and an excellent but unrelated second spin-off before plummeting headlong into a savage decline, resurrected fairly well in the Nineties with *Halloween H20*. Wes Craven's (c.f.) *A Nightmare On Elm Street* went from surreal and visceral dream master to "please tell me it's just a bad dream" disaster, although it too had a brief stay of execution in its most recent incarnation. Even such relatively mediocre box-office performers such as *The Stepfather* (a chilling, influential independent film) had a couple, as did the hugely enjoyable *Tremors*, the downright stupid *Puppet Master* and any number of other killer doll/little people films (*Child's Play*). But pride of place goes to the *Friday The Thirteenth* films. Started in 1980 by Sean Cunningham this nasty, incongruous and tedious slasher produced eight wretched sequels, a dreadful TV spin-off and the ominous promise of more to come.

However, there were still gems out there. Larry Cohen was producing a range of eclectic movies from *Q* (1982), which featured an Aztec god in New York, to *The Stuff* (1986), about killer dessert that comes from the ground, and a *Return To Salem's Lot* (1987), where the vampires snack on coach parties when they think no one's looking.

Another trend that tentatively started in the Seventies and continues to the present day is that of the Stephen King adaptation. His prolific body of work and commercial success has led to virtually anything he has penned turning up in some form on cinema or television screens. From the surprisingly successful low-budget *The Children Of The Corn* (1984), the limp *Cujo* (1983), his own directorial debut *Maximum Overdrive* (1986), and

Creepshow (1982), to television series such as *Salem's Lot* (1979) and *The Stand* (1994), he remains the modern horror film's most influential writer.

The Evil Dead (1982)

Dir: Sam Raimi St: Bruce Campbell

Two guys, three girls. A break in a cabin in the country. Relaxing. Or not. Cut off from civilisation by a rickety bridge, the surrounding woods are host to a mightily evil entity that you really, really wouldn't want to summon, certainly not with an incantation gleaned from a spooky tape recorder and a human-leather bound book. Ooops...

In the UK *The Evil Dead* became one of the most notorious films ever made due to a vitriolic press campaign against it. Such was the furore that it turned up on the DPP's list as one of the original video nasties, a label that has stuck to this day. So is it that bad? Funded by hawking the idea to local businessmen, the entrepreneurial spirit and sheer persistence of the cast and crew involved is breathtaking. The camerawork alone puts many multi-million dollar films to shame, dashing around like a thing possessed, swooping over cars and through the trees, smashing through windows and doors. In realising an unstoppable force, the viewer's vantage point goes beyond that of the voyeur normally associated with horror cinema; there is no cut from the prowl to the attack, the watcher becomes as possessed as the characters. Not content with blistering camerawork Raimi fills his frame with bizarre angles and distorted cartoon figures of fear. The sound is uniformly great throughout, normally the big let-down of low-budget films, with effective use of eerie slowed down tape and indescribable moans. When the group start turning into cackling possessed killers things really start hotting up. Fortunately for gorehounds these demons can only be dispatched by "total bodily dismemberment," so heads are lopped off with spades, bodies chainsawed and all manner of atrocities abound. *The Evil Dead* is problematic for viewers and censors because it is a great film made by dedicated individuals trying to scare the bejeezus out of you. It succeeds, but remains funny too.

Evil Dead 2: Dead By Dawn's (1987) emphasis on *Three Stooges*-style comedy mixed with overt gore makes it a less edgy remake but still a lot of fun. In particular Campbell's performance as Ash has become hyperactive to the point of insanity especially when facing his own homicidal hand. The third film, *Army Of Darkness* (1992) has Ash, caught in the vortex from part two, battling his evil self in a mythic past. Played almost entirely for laughs, the Harryhausen inspired skeletons and painful mini-Ashes go together to produce an amiable fantasy.

The Thing (1982)

Dir: John Carpenter St: Kurt Russell

The idyll of Arctic research is abruptly curtailed by the arrival of a husky, hotly pursued by two wild-eyed gun-toting Norwegians. Man's best friend turns out to be a parasitic pooch, a malevolent mutant mutt created from a prehistoric alien organism that assimilates host cells and occupies its victims. Stranded, the twelve US boys become increasingly twitchy, not knowing who is the thing, and who is its next victim.

John Carpenter's remake of Howard Hawks' *The Thing From Another World* (1956) could not be more different in visual effect. Where the original features a barely glimpsed monster, relying on shadows and implication, Carpenter gleefully plays it all to camera in glorious widescreen colour with added icky bits to go. Based more closely on Campbell's story *Who Goes There?*, *The Thing* replicates its victims so that it can kill again, hiding inside the familiar. To this end no one is above suspicion, MacReady even killing one of his colleagues who we later discover was not possessed. Normally, visceral excess replaces tension in horror films, but Carpenter pulls off both and throws in some substantial jumps - the scene where the group are testing their blood together has provided a template for 'is he/isn't he' tensions in numerous subsequent films. Not that Carpenter shies from plundering the back catalogue of horror films to get the right effect - *Invasion Of The Body Snatchers*, *The Quatermass Experiment* and *The Haunting* all get a look in. What sets it apart are the incredible prosthetics on show; dogs split open and whip around tentacles, human heads consume other human heads, bodies are thrown like rag dolls, burnt, mutilated and eviscerated. There are sticky alien autopsies, frozen suicidal blood and the most jaw-dropping cardiac arrest scene ever. Ennio Morricone provides a score that is Carpenter in all but name and Kurt Russell plays, well, Kurt Russell. Surprisingly this was not a financial success, its reputation developing well after the initial release. Twenty years since its making, it remains a sticky romp and a lean, fun watch.

Spoorloos (The Vanishing) (1988)

Dir: George Sluizer St: Gene Bervoerts, Johanna Ter Steege, Bernard-Pierre Donnadieu

Saskia keeps having dreams about herself and Rex being golden eggs drifting in an empty void. Three years later Rex starts having similar dreams while he is searching for her after she mysteriously disappeared at a motorway service station. His devotion to finding out what happened has cost him dearly, a matter not helped by postcards he receives from a person who claims to know about the vanishing. He is Raymond Lemorne and his role in Saskia's disappearance is even more sinister than his beard. And believe us his beard is decidedly suspect.

Based upon Tim Krabbé's *The Golden Egg* (he also supplied the screenplay), *The Vanishing* is one of the most compelling and disturbing thrillers ever made, lingering in the mind for days after viewing. Yet it contains virtually nothing in its imagery or language to warrant a high rating - it's the psychological effect that is so devastating. The premise is so simple that it is ideally suited to Sluizer's matter of fact direction. (He also edited, co-produced and co-wrote.) This economy of style is deceptive as the film plays havoc with chronology. After Saskia disappears we are formally introduced to Raymond but it is some time before it is made clear that these scenes are set prior to her abduction. There are references to Saskia's dream throughout, although we are unaware until the very end that it is actually a premonition of her fate. Golden eggs are symbolised not only in the lighters that mark the claustrophobic conclusion, but the headlights of cars, the lorry in the tunnel and two buried coins. What also sets the film apart from a run-of-the-mill thriller is the concentration on the act of perpetrating a motiveless crime for the whim of "the spirit of contradiction," ironically where the film gains much of its black humour. Donnadieu's performance is as calculated as his character's intentions, but in keeping with the spirit he is also a figure of contradiction; a loving family man with two daughters ("the only man in France without a mistress") and a good teacher. This attitude makes his self-confessed sociopath behaviour all the more worrying because he is not a dismissable monster or even the product of a traumatised childhood. Subtle, quiet and wholly convincing *Spoorloos* is one of the most memorably nasty of psychological horror films, and there's not a drop of blood spilled.

In an almost inconceivably bad move, Sluizer remade the film in Hollywood five years later with Kiefer Sutherland and a painfully miscast Jeff Bridges. Missing the whole point of the original and changing the ending, this travesty should be avoided at all costs.

My, Aren't We So Postmodern Now: The Nineties

The early Nineties gave little comfort to genre buffs. Censorship on both sides of the pond was beginning to relax slightly but not for horror films. It was kept alive in the straight-to-video market where, in the UK, it suffered more from the censors' wrath due to its perceived availability to children. Instead the action film boomed, as did comedy, and people started asking - why should I watch a few dumb teenagers getting killed when I can watch hundreds of grown men get wasted in a gunplay film? To some extent this question remains unanswered, and although the market for horror did pick up rapidly and remains healthy to this day it is difficult to see how a serious horror film can match the extreme graphic excesses of *Saving Private Ryan* (1998) or *Starship Troopers* (1997). Horror's response was to become subtle (*The Sixth Sense*), slapstick (*Braindead*), steep itself in knowingly self-referential irony (*Scream*) or place itself in such a way that it was not considered a horror film at all (*Se7en*).

The Crow (1994), Brandon Lee's final film, turned the idea of supernatural vengeance on its head by having the wronged spirit back from the dead as the hero of the film. Based on the comic book, its visual extremities and pop video aesthetics would have an impact on far too many MTV-inspired imitators. Similarly Spielberg's *Jurassic Park* (1993) reawakened interest in dinosaurs by using Michael Crichton's genetic reworking of *King Kong* as a basis for PG-rated scares using expensive and groundbreaking special effects. David Fincher's *Se7en* (1995) was an unbearably grim and serious reworking of the Dr Phibes films. Typified by a total absence of humour, Konji's crisply murky chiaroscuro camerawork and emphasis on the after-effects of murder rather than its mechanics, *Se7en* was an unlikely success story.

Realising a gap in the market, screenwriter Kevin Williamson updated the slasher film in a way that would work for a 'seen it all' Nineties audience. Bearing in mind that the main audience for the horror film is 16 to 25-year-olds, the bulk of subgenres can easily accommodate a ten to fifteen-year cycle of resurrection and reinterpretation. To Nineties kids, the 'stalk and slash film' was a product of an earlier age. *I Know What You Did Last Summer* (1997) was a basic reworking of the classic formula - pretty kids, one mistake, nutzoid killer. As with most of its ilk the murderer has a suitable dress code (here a sou'wester) and a modus operandi for the killing spree (a fishhook). The film's success probably had as much to do with its cast as its content, which is little more than a couple of murders and a Scooby Doo ending. However it was with *Scream* that Williamson shot to public attention (c.f. Wes Craven) a distillation of horror trivia, comedy and some genuinely shocking murders. Suddenly postmodern was in, big time. Robert Rodriguez's *The Faculty* (1998) put the fun back into *Invasion Of The Body Snatchers* by mixing it with the ethos of *Buffy The Vampire Slayer,* piling on the gore and icky special effects - its good natured film-making and devil-may-care attitude making a great popcorn movie. *Urban Legend* took the slasher revival to its tedious inevitability by being a tired series of killings based on urban myths.

Not that it was only stalk 'n' slash films that got revived; *The Haunting* (1999) was Jan de Bont's antiseptic remake of Robert Wise's classic that managed to throw away some of the most imaginative set design seen. Far cheaper, nastier and better was *House On Haunted Hill* (1999), a remake of the classic William Castle shocker where a group of guests have to survive the night in an austere futurist haunted house if they are to walk away with one million dollars. The combination of plot turns, surprises and deaths that are faked may well render the film preposterous but the plethora of gruesome happenings and the macabre joie de vivre makes it a far more satisfying, if intellectually undemanding, experience.

Meanwhile, showing that the ultra low-budget film was not a product of the past, the ridiculously cheap *The Blair Witch Project* (1999) was a surprising sleeper hit, prompting the inevitable sequels and an unfortunate number of camcorder horror imitators.

Braindead (1992)

Dir: Peter Jackson St: Timothy Balme, Elizabeth Moody

Lionel is a mummy's boy, it's just that mummy isn't too well. In fact she's dead, infected by the bite of a Simian Raticus. She's in good company, sharing her cellar with an increasing population of braindeads. It's all Lionel can do to keep them fed, sedated and out of trouble, but to expect him to keep up his relationship with pretty Paquita and maintain the lawn-mower in peak condition is asking too much. To make matters worse, odious Uncle Les has decided to throw a party for all his hideous friends.

One of the goriest, most disgusting, entrails-spilling, headchopping splatterfests to get a commercial release, *Braindead* is irresponsible and gratuitously violent. It's also wildly inventive, brilliantly designed and very, very funny. Jackson's previous film, the appropriately named *Bad Taste*, similarly features a phenomenally high gore rating but is essentially a comedy too - the excesses are more Monty Python than Lucio Fulci. *Braindead* improves on this, using better pacing, a stronger script and a

Fifties setting. Heritage splatter New Zealand style, with loads of references to Her Majesty and *The Archers*. Never one to keep the camera still, and always choosing the most grotesque angles with which to fill the screen, Jackson ensures the audience stay on their toes. His characters are all larger than life, from the pasty faced mother with her diminishing number of appendages, the vigilante vicar who "kicks arse for the lord" before becoming a very randy zombie, the accommodating nurse with the almost detachable head and the truly disgusting Uncle Les - and he's still alive! There are so many comic and gross sequences, but the highlight comes when Lionel takes the zombie baby for a pram ride in the park. When the party gets into full swing the violence reaches astronomical levels; half heads slide around the floor like pucks, whole ribcages are wrenched from bodies, heads split open, entrails strangle the living and the place is so awash with bodily fluids that Lionel can't run because the floor is so slippery. But even that is topped by the outrageously Oedipal ending. If this sounds revolting, it's because it is, but it is made with such impish glee you end up grinning wildly at every new atrocity. Fortunately the BBFC saw the joke and released the film uncut, but the MPAA had a serious humour bypass, savagely reducing the film's running time. Sacrilege. Jackson went on to make the remarkable *Heavenly Creatures* (1994) and the effects-heavy horror-comedy *The Frighteners*.

Dust Devil (1995)

Dir: Richard Stanley St: Robert Burke, Chelsea Field

In Namibia bodies are discovered with signs of ritualistic abuse. They are the work of a Nagtloper, a shape shifter who "feeds from the damned and sucks them dry," bound in flesh to walk the material world. Wendy has just ditched her husband and is heading towards the sea to sort out her life when she picks up the Dust Devil, putting herself at the mercy of a power far greater than she can possibly imagine.

Richard Stanley's enjoyable sf horror *Hardware* proved he could make effective and impressive films on a pitiful budget and its success gave him the opportunity to film a pet project, *Dust Devil*. Filming in Namibia was harsh and the film's troubled distribution came very close to complete failure were it not for the director's determination to self-finance a new print in line with his vision. And what a vision it is. The Nagtloper travels to places where magic is still believed, finding itself in the harsh but painfully beautiful desert. Its very existence lies in the cruelty and suddenness of the wind, its purpose is entirely ritualistic and the modern world cannot explain its primitive brutality. His first victim is killed mid-coitus. Her neck snapped, he divides her body into ritualistically determined portions, daubs the house in bloody glyphs, inserts a pocket watch into her, takes her fingers and torches the pad. Even Ben, a sceptical police officer, realises immediately that he is going to need the help of a Sangomas (a kind of shaman) who provides him with a totem that will banish the demon. Ben and Wendy, our central characters, question the existence of the supernatural, but accept it because their environment forces this as a logical explanation. Wendy's romantic relationship with the Dust Devil begins when he explains the creation of the land "home of the great snake father... created by the thrashing of his coils" as the camera performs an astonishing helicopter shot to show the two of them as insignificant dots amidst a sublime landscape. The climax is set inside a ghost town, the ending playing on the theme of Leone's classic westerns but Stanley imbues the Western mythology with magick symbolism. This relies upon the cessation of pain and exact timing, the Dust Devil's pocket watches providing further credence to the malleability of time. While there are many allusions to other horror films *Dust Devil* is one of a kind - unflinching, grim, mythical and intelligent. Shot with a glowing intensity that feels gritty yet otherworldly, it sticks in the mind long after the credits have rolled.

The Blair Witch Project (1999)

Dir: Daniel Myrick, Eduardo Sanchez St: Heather Donahue, Michael Williams, Joshua Leonard

Three amateur film-makers decide to make a documentary about the Blair Witch. Boy were they wrong. All that remains of their lame-brained idea is an abandoned bundle of video tapes and some arty-farty 16mm black and white stuff. But who were they? Heather, brains behind the project; Josh, photographer; Mike, hyper-tense soundman. Together they traipse through the Maryland forests but pretty soon become lost, unable to escape back to their car. Food requires rationing and their night-time camping becomes disturbed by the sounds of screaming children and unidentified noises without apparent source. Piles of stones and twig effigies appear outside their tents. Tempers fray. Josh disappears leaving what appears to be a small lump of flesh while Mike and Heather descend further into desperation and further into the forest.

The hype surrounding *The Blair Witch Project*, with its carefully orchestrated advertising campaign through the internet make it, in percentage terms, the most successful horror film of all time, partly down to the ridiculously low-budget. As a concept and experiment the film is flawless and the acting surprisingly effective - we are led to believe the story because of the way the directors manipulated the actors and kept them up all night - the heartfelt sobbing is decidedly uncomfortable. This creates a sense of intimacy and claustrophobia with no possibility for distancing from the action short of someone putting their camera down. That the three film-makers who shot it have disappeared seeks further to convince you that events portrayed are genuine. The twig effigies are intriguing and provide the film with its most arresting images, especially in the sequence where we see them hanging ominously from trees, shot in 16mm black and white to make a startling contrast to the grainy video footage. However, despite this, and a subtle and implicitly nasty ending, *Blair Witch* fails to be a good horror film because it's just not scary. In the cinema the handheld camerawork is far more nausea-inducing than the scenes of terror, it really should have been unleashed straight to video where ultimately it has more resonance. An interesting idea, dreamt up by ad-men (and as vacuous), the end results are mildly diverting and no more. A modestly (as opposed to no) budgeted sequel ditched the experimental approach and emerged as a deeply dull post-*Scream* self-referential yawnfest. How post-post-modernly ironic. How dated. How Nineties.

Ten Terrifying Auteurs

Horror is one of the few genres which positively encourages the auteur. When compiling a list of the best, one has to remember those talented directors that didn't quite make it – Roger Corman, Tobe Hooper, John Carpenter, Peter Jackson and Sam Raimi who have been omitted mainly for reasons of space, but also because some have produced spectacular films within other genres as well. We have tried to cover their work elsewhere in the book, because they are emphatically worth watching for their horror output.

Tod Browning (1882–1962)

Charles Albert (aka Tod) Browning was one of America's first horror auteurs, a man whose affinity for the grotesque led him to direct a number of key genre films, although strangely his most renowned work is by no means his best. After leaving home Browning joined a carnival as a macabre side-show attraction 'The Living Hypnotic Corpse' where he would remain in state, buried underground for people to gawp at. He became involved with DW Griffiths, initially as an actor but later as an assistant on the epic *Intolerance* (1916). This experience led him to write and direct a series of adventure, melodrama and western serials before finding his true vocation - horror. *The Wicked Darling* (1919) was the first of many feature-length collaborations with the great actor Lon Chaney, 'The Man With a Thousand Faces.' Chaney had perfected the art of gruesome make-up to transform himself into some of cinema's most hideous, and occasionally sympathetic figures, often at great personal discomfort. The pair clicked in their ideas of representing internal psychological torment with external physicality, appearances becoming as much representational as actual. *The Unholy Three* (1925) features three carnival renegades, a dwarf, a strongman and an occasionally transvestite ventriloquist (Chaney) arranging a cunning jewel heist, each adapting his unique skills to the task at hand. *The Blackbird* (1926) and *The Road To Mandalay* (1926) followed, but more deranged is *The Unknown* (1927) where Chaney plays a knife thrower in love with a radiant Joan Crawford. Doesn't sound too strange? Well Joan rebukes his advances causing our unhinged cutlery chucker to spiral downwards into murder and self-abuse, culminating (some sixty years prior to Jodorowsky's dazzling *Santa Sangre*) in a last bid attempt for her affections by amputating both of his arms. *London After Midnight* (1927) was Browning's foray into the vampire genre with a top-hatted, cloaked Chaney sporting a distorted mouthful of excruciatingly painful canine incisors that ripped his face into a demonic grin. It made Chaney the ideal choice to play *Dracula* but sadly he passed away in 1930 (his son adopted the name and carried on the family business, most memorably in a series of werewolf pictures) and the part went to Bela Lugosi, who had played the role on stage. *Dracula* has moments of macabre brilliance but it is clear that Browning's heart was not entirely in the project. The success of the film launched the cycle of Universal horror films and gave Browning virtual carte blanche over his next project, this time for MGM, a studio not known for pushing the boundaries of acceptability. And what a project it was. *Freaks* gave the studio exactly what they asked for but not what they wanted, a horror film. Considered impossible to release (especially in light of the Hays Code) the film was shelved with disgust and considerable disbelief. Browning's career never really recovered although his final films do maintain sparks of his former works. *Mark Of The Vampire* (1935), a convoluted but highly enjoyable vampire thriller, features incredibly dense set dressing and lush, stylised photography. Lugosi is at his finest, bone-white succubus bride by his side wandering through his cobwebbed castle or fog-bound patios. Ostensibly a remake of *London After Midnight,* the astonishing effects work, the Gothic grandeur and expressive sweeping camerawork are sadly offset by some ill-conceived comedy sequences and a disappointingly rational conclusion. *The Devil Doll* (1936) saw Lionel Barrymore as a vengeful banker instigating terrible revenge on his deceitful and crooked partners. He does this, occasionally in cunning drag disguises, using miniaturised humans.

Browning's sympathy with disadvantaged protagonists sees resonance in the films of Tim Burton, as does his eye for the trappings of Gothic melodrama. Although he made films in many genres his legacy remains in the few sound horror films he made in the Thirties. Unfortunately his eclectic visions clashed with the sensibilities of the age and he ceased making films in 1939.

Dracula (1930)

Dir: Tod Browning St: Bela Lugosi, Dwight Frye, David Manners, Helen Chandler

Renfield travels to Transylvania to sell Carfax Abbey to Count Dracula, who makes him subservient to his will. As a result, upon his return to England, Renfield is incarcerated at Dr Seward's home for the criminally insane. Dr Seward and his daughter Mina meet their strange new neighbour at the opera. When Mina's friend Lucy dies though, resident stake bearer Abraham Van Helsing decides that something must be done...

The success and influence of *Dracula* is so enormous that it is genuinely difficult to view objectively. Without doubt though, it will be forever remembered for Dracula himself. Lugosi had already played the role on stage and despite not being first choice for the lead, the Hungarian actor was made for the part. He played a very different vampire to the more visceral Chaney emphasising a doomed, romantic edge that would endear him to female fans the world over. He draws the eye with raw power and considerable charm - when he attacks men he is a savage to fear, with women he is a passionate lover. Individual sequences remain enormously powerful even now, and the mise en scène is nothing short of astonishing. Dracula's castle is a huge cathedral-like hall with streaming light, a dizzying staircase, colossal spiders' webs and, inexplicably, armadillos. There are lashings of ideas at the start – the bat-led carriage and the ghostly brides stalking Renfield being of particular note. However, when the action moves to England, it feels as though Browning has simply run out of steam, relying on off-screen action and a good deal of exposition relayed through dialogue, rather than continuing with the stunning visual ideas promised at the start.

Freaks (1932)

Dir: Tod Browning St: Harry Earles, Olga Baclanova, Daisy Earles

Circus life. Midgets Hans and Frieda are all set to marry but Hans falls for the manipulative, beautiful and 'regular' sized trapeze artist Cleo(patra). Cleo is just after his substantial fortune, formulating a plan with Hercules the strongman - she will wed Hans and slowly poison him. But the callous couple don't reckon on the strength of community spirit that exists among the gentler circus folk for if you "offend one then you offend them all," and believe me, they are mightily offended...

Some films have reputations that precede them but few have the fierce reaction that *Freaks* possesses. It was shelved by a disgusted studio, condemned by the few who saw it and banned for decades in the UK. Even the titles find their way into the narrative space by being ripped open in front of our eyes, before being hyped up by the master of ceremonies who relates the tale in flashback. What makes Browning's masterpiece so inflammatory is that the 'freaks' are genuine, not some product of make-up and this forces the viewer to reinterpret their aloof position - they are shown as normal people living out their lives. Films of side-show unfortunates were not new but up until *Freaks*, and sadly afterwards as well, they existed in the realm of monster movies or as casual scares. *Freaks* does not allow the audience the luxury of distancing themselves from their emotions and lifestyles - ultimately it was this that offended everyone at the time. It is easier to dismiss them as grotesque side-show entertainment than contemplate the horror of an active loving mind being subjected to the casual cruelty of the gawping public. Even more shocking is the way in which these loving people can turn into monsters, albeit temporarily, when one of their comrades is threatened. With such an inflammatory title, the real freaks of the piece are Hercules and Cleo, uncaring, shallow, and deformed on the inside, defined entirely by lust, both sexual and financial. The traditionally marginalised characters are more complex and rounded. The film refuses to become polemic or simplistic, both Venus and Phroso are basically beautiful people, but are as much part of the community as anyone and a million miles removed from the scheming duo. Even if the narrative hook, the extortion of Hans at the expense of his true love, were removed you would still be left with a fascinating insight into circus life and culture. Browning, you will recall, spent some years in a circus and this is apparent in the mundane representation of life behind the glitz; lives, loves, breaks, gambling, practising, preparing new clown gags, stagehands ogling the girls, it's all here. Importantly we never see anyone perform, or see their audiences. In some ways we have impinged on their world by being granted this intimate viewpoint. Insightful, moving and compassionate, *Freaks* is a beautiful if harsh work that has few peers. Its influence on, for example, David Lynch's *The Elephant Man* is profound.

James Whale (1889–1957)

Initially, James Whale pursued a career as an actor in Britain, but found his talents drew him into theatrical set design and eventually direction. His experiences in World War I made him the ideal choice to direct a stage version of the controversial anti-war play *Journey's End* by RC Sherriff, concerning the futile loss of young life in the trenches. The success of the production was such that he was asked over to Hollywood, serving as dialogue director for Howard Hughes on *Hell's Angels* (1930) before getting the chance to direct his first feature, reprising his theatre success with a modest adaptation of *Journey's End* (1930). *Waterloo Bridge* (1931) followed but his big break came with *Frankenstein*, the first of four horror films he made for Universal which sky-rocketed ex-vaudeville actor Boris Karloff (Henry Pratt) into A-list territory. The influence of German expressionism on his visual style is apparent in the sets and feel of his films, but is tempered by softer use of camerawork and composition. Whale's jarring visuals come predominantly from his occasionally shocking use of editing and attention to set detail rather than the distortion of his narrative space through camerawork. He relies on fluid movements to immerse the viewer into scenes. Given free reign he produced the wickedly funny *Old Dark House*. Staying firmly in Blighty (at least in setting) *The Invisible Man* (1933) introduced Claude Rains as the titular scientist and set him on the road to stardom, no mean feat as he spends virtually the entire time wrapped in bandages or not there at all! The film's playful visual nature worked perfectly against the darker areas of the script, offering little hope of redemption as Rains descends into madness and eventually death, appearing fully just in time to catch the end titles. Not only is this a succinct, amusing and poignant film but it also boasts some of the most technically advanced special effects of the time; bottles are thrown by invisible hands, shirts dance in mockery of the townsfolk out to lynch him, bikes ride apparently without rider and Rains reveals himself by creepily unwrapping his bandages, uncovering frightening nothingness. For some sequences the black matted shirt collars and cuffs that run across the screen were hand-touched frame by frame to disguise the effect (a similar technique would be used to remove the wires from Linda Blair's levitation scene in *The Exorcist*). The film's success led to many sequels and spin-offs but none have the eccentric, macabre charm and wit of the original. *The Bride Of Frankenstein* (1935) continued his successful streak, remaining his most often emulated film, homages of which can be seen even today. It was to be the last horror film he would direct although much of his later work contained the same love of morbid humour or sympathising with the misunderstood or eccentric. The musical *Show Boat* (1936) showed the compassionate but occasionally cruel side of his work. *Remember Last Night?* (1936) was a witty and very sick thriller where the usual parlour gathering of aristocrats have to solve a murder. What sets it apart from the run-of-the-mill mystery is that they are drunk. He went on to direct *The Man In The Iron Mask* (1939) and an early Vincent Price vehicle *Green Hell* (1940). Sadly, disagreements with Universal forced Whale into retirement in 1941.

Frankenstein (1931)

Dir: James Whale St: Colin Clive, Boris Karloff, Edward van Sloan

Henry Frankenstein has got it all: a beautiful fiancée, a hereditary title, and a place in Goldstadt Medical College. Why then should he throw it all away and shack up with a sadistic hunchback called Fritz with poor brain-napping skills and a sideline in gratuitous eye rolling? Simple, Henry is raiding the graves and gallows of the land to create a new being. His creation is a success but his paternal skills are somewhat lacking and the confused, vengeful beast escapes to terrorise the community.

Whale's film opens in wonderful showman style with a warning that what we are about to witness "might even horrify you," a truly melodramatic touch. For such a short film this naturally takes enormous liberties with Mary Shelley's novel but as a story in its own right it stands up rather well, especially the sequences where the deranged duo stalk evocative graveyards as they acquire the monster's requisite body parts. The tight framing and morbid statues eke every morsel of ghoulish dread from the viewer but at heart the film remains a comedy, albeit a very black one. Skeletons bounce on rubber bands, dirt is shovelled unceremoniously over monuments and much fun is to be had with any cadaver that pops into view. Henry's assistant Fritz is the archetypal lumbering companion, relentlessly stupid, grovelling and sadistic. When retrieving a brain from the medical college, this hapless hunchback not only smashes the one marked 'Normal,' he even swaps it with the one marked 'Abnormal' and neglects to tell the boss.

Karloff's performance as The Monster (with groundbreaking make-up by Jack Pierce that is synonymous with the creature's look even today) ranges from wild gesticulations to moments of poignancy. Despite his brutality, we retain a great deal of sympathy with him. In the film's finest scene (sadly censored in many prints) The Monster is shown innocent companionship in the shape of Maria, a little girl. They play with flowers, making them float in the river but the creature, inspired by the simplistic beauty of the drifting petals, throws the girl to a watery grave.

The film's influence was immense, particularly with Frankenstein becoming a cultural icon - recognisable seventy years on, his legacy on film goes far beyond the scope of 'mere' horror. Mel Brooks' pastiche *Young Frankenstein* (1974) is a comedic love letter to Whale, even filming in black and white and using the original sets (found in the designer's garage after forty years!) while the *Spirit Of The Beehive* (1973) uses the film as a political metaphor and a gentle tale of growing up in the shadow of tyranny.

The Old Dark House (1932)

Dir: James Whale St: Boris Karloff, Melvyn Douglas, Charles Laughton, Raymond Massey

Torrential rainfall and devastating landslides strand Mr & Mrs Waverton and their companion Penderel far from Shrewsbury. Their only source of shelter is an old dark house with its unhinged inhabitants the Femms and the sinister Morgan. Self-made businessman Sir William Porterhouse, and his chorus girl 'friend' Gladys join the unusual throng and suspicions begin to run rife as to who, or what, is living on the third floor...

From the lightening strike that announces Whale's name on the title cards you know that this is not going to be a serious ride. Adapting J B Priestley's novel, the screenplay for *The Old Dark House* gives the rapid, droll, black dialogue of Edwardian writing its first decent cinematic airing, and Whale's direction never shies from being scary at the same time. Dark is definitely the operative word, much of the film taking place by stuttering electric light ("We make our own electric light out here, only we aren't very good at it") or flickering candle, where the shadows 'act' as much the actors. Whale lets his performers and script tell the story, but peppers proceedings with some genuinely frightening set pieces. The variations in the characters' personae as they progress from apparently normal to deranged is emphasised by wonderfully low-key lighting. Morgan, the scar-faced alcoholic half-mute ("Even Welsh shouldn't sound like that") is an uncivilised beast, but he's also a handy electrician and makes an excellent joint of beef. Horace Femm is wonderfully camp, paranoid and droll in contrast to his sister's wailing fanaticism. Saul is perfectly balanced as a sympathetic madman with a destructive streak in homicide and pyromania. That ultimately the family turn out to be just highly unusual is the final irony - all the ostensibly 'normal' characters are either promiscuous, vacuous or spend their normal lives bickering about trivialities. Despite being a Universal picture, this is as British as a stiff upper lip, playing upon excruciating interest in the minutiae of climate change and not saying what you mean. Whale manages to find plenty of opportunity to relish in the rampant decadence of an age in decline - with hellfire and brimstone dialogue about sin, a very risqué mutual seduction and some of the most outrageous foot fetishism outside of Buñuel's work. Later Universal horror comedies, while enjoyable, tended to concentrate on slapstick or puns. *The Old Dark House* is far more acerbic and subtle than any of these, even finding time to pastiche *Jane Eyre*.

Bride Of Frankenstein (1935)

Dir: James Whale St: Boris Karloff, Colin Clive, Elsa Lanchester

It's alive! The monster has escaped the burning windmill while, back in town, a woozy Frankenstein is atoning for his misdemeanours. Not for long though, as silver-tongued madman Dr Pretorious and his jam jars of miniature people persuade the baron that his errant creation needs a good woman to propagate a new race, a "world of gods and monsters." The pair get straight to work...

Only four years after the original stormed the screen but the changes are immense. Karloff (single word) is given a pre-title credit showing that perhaps the monster has become bigger than its creator. Rapid advances in camera technology allowed Whale the freedom to employ gliding shots, with plenty of opportunity to caress the huge soft-expressionist sets and take in every wind-billowed gossamer dress. Most of the special effects work is highly believable, Dr Pretorious' little people are blended seamlessly with the actors in a manner that is quite astonishing. He steals much of the limelight from Frankenstein, who is currently wracked with remorse, because Pretorious is quite obviously insane.

However the effects of the Hays code become all too evident, the gallows humour of the original is still there but not as voracious - becoming more slapstick than macabre - "I need to speak with you on a grave matter." Likewise, the introduction has become a camp explanation of the story's moral validity, emphasising the religious points in an attempt to curtail censorship. That said, the cruel slaughter of little Maria's parents at the film's opening is as grimly funny as it is brutal and unjust. The Monster too is far less ambiguous - he clearly just wants the respect of others. When he catches sight of his reflection for the first time he is repulsed but begins to accept his right to be different when shown the joy of friendship with a companion who is also an outsider. Events gallop along at a cracking pace, the Monster is only incarcerated for about twenty seconds before he has wrenched free from his shackles and barged the door down in 'big id' fashion. That the climax is so abrupt is more than another joke, it's a necessity that allows the tantalisingly brief images to stay in the mind. Elsa Lanchester's appearance as the bride is so stunning it eclipses virtually everything else we've been shown, a Gothic fantasy of pale skin, hospital robe wedding dress, impossible hair and delicate mapwork of surgery scars. Although filled with breathtaking imagery and excellent effects work, *Bride Of Frankenstein* falls just short of its forebear by replacing single-focused fableism with unnecessarily explicit moralising.

Val Lewton (1904–1951)

Traditionally theories of authorship have concentrated on the director as guiding force when considering a canon of work. Val Lewton however, is best known as a producer. What makes his work so interesting is not only do the films bear the hallmarks of the directors who made them but that they also remain irrefutably Lewton's. Born Vladimir Leventon his family emigrated to the US from Yalta, Russia, when he was five, changing their name to Lewton. Thanks to his mother Nina he landed a job in Hollywood as story editor and general writer for, amongst others, David O Selznick. In 1942 he was approached by RKO Radio Pictures, who were going through a bit of a lean patch. Needing to recoup costs they hit upon the idea of producing cheap horror films as the minor parts of double bills. B-Features received a percentage of the takings so providing the initial budget was low enough, they couldn't fail to make money. All Lewton's unit had to do was keep the length down and they were pretty much left alone - with one additional proviso that the studio would choose the title based on market research. Thus the Lewton produced films have provocative titles and often sensationalist posters yet paradoxically remain the most lyrical or poetic films of the genre. Lewton's role in the making of these films is far greater than his producer status would suggest. He often provided the inspiration for the tales, the literary aspects of the scripting, taking co-screenwriting credits occasionally under the pseudonym Carlos Keith and certainly imbued the films with their feel, tone and style. It helped to have such talented people working for him - Lewton's films were nothing if not collaborative efforts. Lewton gave three directors their first major stabs at the craft and all would serve him well.

Jacques Tourneur had made short films and produced some second unit work in both the US and France but the job of directing *Cat People* (1942), the unit's first film, was his first major feature. Critically and financially successful it was followed by the evocative *I Walked With A Zombie* (1943), a beautifully shot elegiac piece based in part on *Jane Eyre*. This was Lewton's trump card, instead of relying on penny dreadful horrors or fairy-tale thrillers he turned to literary and artistic precedents for the screenplays - the works of Bronte and Stephenson, psychoanalytic theory and the poetry of Milton and Shakespeare. The yearning meanderings in *I Walked With A Zombie* invoke an ethereal yet harsh romantic world far detached from the standard B-movie pot-boiler. So impressed were RKO with Tourneur's work that they promised him A-list status should he complete a third film. *The Leopard Man* (1943) was again full of the hints of exotic ritual, superstition and folk tale undercurrents. After leaving the RKO horror unit Tourneur made a substantial number of films noirs and westerns (including the wonderful *Build My Gallows High* (1947)), returning to horror for *Night Of The Demon* (1957), a taut intelligent working of M R James' *Casting The Runes* with glowing black and white cinematography.

Both Mark Robson and Robert Wise had worked as editors prior to their association with Lewton, collaborating on Orson Welles' *Citizen Kane* (1941) and *The Magnificent Ambersons* (1942). Robson had joined as an editor on *Cat People* but Lewton was determined to put him behind the camera, even at the expense of his own promotion. *The Seventh Victim* (1943) features sumptuously shot sets amid mysterious satanic happenings in Greenwich Village. *Ghost Ship* (1943) features a series of bizarre yet atmospheric deaths aboard a ship captained by the paranoid Dix. *Youth Runs Wild* (1944) was a departure for the unit but with *Isle Of The Dead* (1945) Robson returned to the genre with a vengeance. Set on an isolated and plague-ridden island, from the opening mist-clad shots of cartloads of corpses being carelessly dragged to mass graves, the putrefied air never clears. The primary concept is that one of the characters suffers from acute narcolepsy and at one point is found apparently dead. The camera lingers on her coffin as water drips rhythmically on its lid before finally an extended piercing scream is let out. It is one of the most horrific moments filmed and yet there is nothing to see. Robson's final film for the unit was *Bedlam*, a dense humourless offering with almost inconceivably highbrow dialogue. He later went on to direct the disaster movie *Earthquake* (1974) but his finest films remain understated and steeped in charnel house sensibilities.

Robert Wise co-directed (with Gunther Fritsch) the sequel to Lewton's original hit, *The Curse Of The Cat People* (1944). Oliver has remarried and now has a daughter Amy but the child's insular nature leads to concerns that she is similarly cursed. *The Body Snatcher* suffered the wrath of the BBFC's shears. Wise went on to make an extraordinary range of prestigious films in a wide variety of genres including *The Day The Earth Stood Still* (1951) an impressive science fiction film about the perils of human impetuosity and militarism, as well as two fine musicals *West Side Story* (1961) and *The Sound Of Music* (1965). In 1963 he returned to horror with *The Haunting*, still the finest haunted house film committed to celluloid, with its 'what you don't see' ethos and peerless black and white cinematography.

Ultimately, the success of the horror unit led to Lewton becoming a producer of non-genre flicks, but the results were not as successful due to increasing studio interference. Much of the eloquence that had run through his earlier films was excised in favour of box-office friendly simplicity. Sadly deteriorating health led to an untimely death in 1951. Lewton's influence on the psychological thriller and expressive use of language and literary screenplays mark him as one of the more unusual figures of the field, but one whose work has made it a far richer and more stimulating place.

Cat People (1942)

Dir: Jacques Tourneur St: Simone Simon, Kent Smith, Jane Randolph, Tom Conway

Irena's Serbian background has led her to believe that she is descended from a village of satanic witches and, when aroused, she will turn into a lethal cat-woman. Marriage therefore seems like a pretty bad idea but she ties the knot anyway with Oliver Reed. However her desire to be "really Mrs Reed" is at odds with her fear of lycanthropic savagery and their marriage is unconsummated. A solution in the arms of sinister psychiatrist (and woefully poor keeper of confidentiality) Dr Judd is doomed to failure. Meanwhile hubby Oliver turns to his colleague Alice whose love for him has generated the wrong kind of feline attention.

"When you speak of the soul you mean the mind," despairs Irena at her decidedly creepy psychiatrist, and she is right. She represents the raw emotional passion of the exotic European female in the cold light of the scientifically logical American - her frigidity just as much down to the difference in cultural outlook as childhood trauma. Whatever the cause and whether she is a shapeshifter or not, the fact remains that the tragedy and pathos in *Cat People* is entirely sexual. Perhaps it is Irena's mystique and mood swings that make her such a fascinating subject, the twinkle in her eye, playing with the dead bird and feeding it to the panther - the need for destruction. Tourneur is a master of light and shadow, evoking the claustrophobia of Irena's world with tight, minimal lighting - especially on the psychiatrist's couch, an oval face picked out in a dark void. Wisely the question as to whether Irena really is capable of becoming a panther is left in some doubt - despite the climax there are elements of uncertainty that keep the matter open-ended. Her tragic demise is foreshadowed from the very start, her drawings of an impaled panther at the zoo mirror not only her own death but also relate to the legend of King John and her fears about sexual penetration.

The tension is at times unbearable, the anticipation is far more engaging than the act. Alice being stalked by Irena on her way home is a superb piece of editing and camerawork, keeping you on the edge of the seat, the conclusion with the bus will make you jump a mile high, juxtaposing animal and vehicular sounds to great effect. The scene in the swimming pool is, if anything, even more tense as a vulnerable Alice looks around her to see marbled pool reflections on the walls and hears the unmistakable sounds of hungry predators. The horror of the unseen can be a double-edged sword, when done properly the results are mesmerising and terrifying, but occasionally the audience can feel cheated. *Cat People* never cheats and provides tragedy and sympathy along with the scares. It was remade in a far more graphic and incestuous manner by Paul Schrader in 1982.

The Body Snatcher (1945)

Dir: Robert Wise St: Boris Karloff, Bela Lugosi

Edinburgh, 1831. A city in the stranglehold of graverobbers so that even grieving dogs aren't safe. There is a purpose to all this nefarious necro-napping because the pilfered cadavers are put to good use as doctors' training aids. Dr McFarlan is one such man who uses Gray's dark services, something his new assistant is having a moral crisis over. But when little Georgina needs an operation he relents, realising the worth of the resurrectionist's trade, even if his first delivery seems a touch familiar and a bit too warm...

In adapting Robert Louis Stephenson's story Lewton has helped craft one of his more morally complex screenplays, asking the question of whether distasteful and distressing acts can actually result in good. Our feelings are meant to lie with the young doctor, but it is the other characters embroiled in the sordid business that are far more interesting. Dr McFarlan is brusque and irritable - chiding Georgina he appears devoid of feeling. But he develops from uncaring (it takes long enough to establish that his housekeeper is really his wife) to psychotic, ready to kill in order to save. Perhaps this is due to his unbreakable link with Gray, the creepy cabman and night-time body snatcher. Gray is a complicated character, clearly motivated by greed and impervious to the feelings of those whose graves he desecrates. Nonetheless, he provides a service that will eventually benefit humankind. Matters turn, however, when he murders the singer just to supply her body and we realise just how far he is willing to go. But without him Georgina would never have been cured, not only because of his night job and direct request to Dr McFarlan, but for the kindness he shows her in the shape of Freddie the horse - this gives her hope that motivates her far more than the doctor ever could. Karloff is icy and callous in his portrayal which makes the reduction of Lugosi to a snivelling lackey a sad sight, murdered when he tries to blackmail Gray. Wise wisely (so to speak) keeps his direction underplayed, to allow the subtleties of the script to shine - when the street singer is killed we just watch Gray's coach slowly move to the archway and her voice stops mid-verse. Much of the film's visual sensi-

59

bilities are based around fogging instead of focusing to give a muggy feel to the piece, accentuating the sense of dread. Gray's snuffing technique is shown in matter-of-fact detail, but the censors had most problems with the dialogue. The UK print was heavily excised to remove any reference to Dr Knox, Burke and Hare, quite some feat as Dr McFarlan emphasises several times that he was actually Knox's assistant.

Bedlam (1946)

Dir: Mark Robson St: Boris Karloff, Anna Lee, Billy House

At St Mary's Of Bethlehem they put on one helluva show, releasing the loonies from their cages to perform ineptly for the aristocracy. It's a real hoot. You can even get your own tour for tuppence courtesy of Simms, the Apothecary General. Nell Bowen, companion to the rumbustious Lord Mortimer, finds Simms' treatment of the inmates abominable, so she's quite clearly insane. Best lock her up with the rest of 'em so she can pursue her exercise in compassion as a non-paying guest at... Bedlam.

Robson's (he also co-wrote) uncomfortable portrayal of life in the notorious asylum is unusual in that its source material is a painting by Hogarth. This may go some way to explain the overly static camerawork that frames events rather than immerses the viewer. It may be unsubtle in its political liberalism, but the scale of things necessitate a certain grandeur to nail home the message - greed and power should never be allowed to dominate compassion for a fellow man. To this end, the unlikely pair of heroes are a feisty principled woman and a pacifist Quaker. Nell's convictions see her move from upper society to evicted campaigner to an incarcerated Florence Nightingale figure, tending the pain of the abused inmates. She even questions her own values when she becomes accepted into the 'Pillar Society' that represents the asylum's elite. The villains of the piece distance themselves from their atrocities by denying that the inmates have any humanity in them; they are free to mock, prod and amuse themselves at the often pitiful actions of the 'loonies.' Simms, played with corpse-faced severity and hair-pieced vanity by Karloff, is one of cinema's most consummate sadists, treating his 'guests' worse than any caged animal. Unlike the ignorant, uncaring gawpers who part with their tuppences to ogle the inmates, Simms derives pleasure from their misery. Robson's films may lack the pacy edge of other Lewton stablemates, but he compensates with an immensely flowery script and attention to detail - the stuttering of the dying gold boy, the ripped dress used to tend the wounds of a man in irons, or the remarkable shot of pleading arms bursting from the darkness of their cells. The trial scene at the end plays like a homage to Lang's *M* and the premise of an exposé of abuse in asylums formed the basis for Sam Fuller's *Shock Corridor* (1963).

Terence Fisher (1904-1980)

Perhaps the most famous of Hammer's directors, Terence Fisher began his prolific career in 1947 when he directed a number of low-budget fillers. These included *Colonel Bogey, Stolen Face, Four Sided Triangle, The Astonished Heart* with Noel Coward and *So Long At The Fair*. However, he shot to fame in 1957 with Hammer's first colour gothic film *The Curse Of Frankenstein*. It starred Peter Cushing as the dapper but immoral aristocrat scientist and Christopher Lee as the strangely sympathetic monster. The collaboration of Fisher with scriptwriter Jimmy Sangster and producer Anthony Hinds created a team that would go on to further commercial and artistic glories. All five were reunited for Hammer's next outing *The Horror Of Dracula* (1958) which starred Lee in his best-known role. Sangster's daring script deviates wildly from Stoker's novel, but this is of no consequence; the film is exciting, bold and dramatic. The climax depicting Cushing chasing the increasingly elusive Lee, highlights Fisher's superb pacing of the action - true edge-of-the-seat stuff punctuated by some excruciating comic relief moments. Surprisingly erotic and violent it is an absolute must-see. *The Revenge Of Frankenstein* followed in 1958, this time with Cushing creating a monster from Michael Gwynne. *Frankenstein Created Woman* (1966) sees Frankenstein come to terms with the nature of the soul. In *Frankenstein Must Be Destroyed* (1969) the brain of mad Dr Brandt is transplanted into nice Dr Richter. Fisher plays upon the tragic nature of a monster realising that he is a monster and still recognising his previous life. The last film in the series was the much maligned but brilliant *Frankenstein And The Monster From Hell* (1973). Knowingly comedic and gross it features Frankenstein in an asylum, ostensibly a patient, but in fact carrying on his dastardly deeds, creating a creature assembled from various bits of inmates only to have it torn apart by a lunatic mob.

Continuing with vampires, *Brides Of Dracula* (1960) did not feature Dracula himself, but his disciple Baron Meinster, although Peter Cushing reprised Van Helsing's character. This is an energetic romp with an astonishing climax - Cushing receives a vampire's bite only to cauterise it himself before racing on to destroy the Baron. Christopher Lee returned for *Dracula, Prince Of Darkness*.

Many of Fisher's films were produced quickly (sometimes two or three a year), but his flair for visual style, bold use of strong colours and sense of dramatic pacing ensured that no matter how familiar the story or monster, the finished film would have merit - *The Hound Of The Baskervilles* (1959), *The Mummy* (1959), *The Curse Of The Werewolf* (1960), *The Two Faces Of Dr Jekyll* (1960) and *The Phantom Of The Opera* (1962) were among the best of his output. The same cannot be said for the lamentable *Stranglers Of Bombay*, where a sect commit all manner of atrocities in India. Fisher also directed *The Man Who Could Cheat Death* around this time.

From the mid-Sixties his output decelerated in quantity. *The Gorgon* (1963) scripted by John Gilling, featured Peter Cushing as a doctor whose assistant falls for the last of the Gorgons and Christopher Lee as the cool professor investigating the deaths. Another gothic and melodramatic horror, again the climax is thrilling and not afraid to defy cinematic conventions – you are never sure who is going to survive. *The Horror Of It All* (1963) was a horror comedy set in an old dark house. *The Devil Rides Out* (1967), based upon a Dennis Wheatley novel, was not a commercial hit but has gathered cult status over the years. Set much later than the Gothic horrors and combining brilliantly saturated colour and lighting with precise camerawork and editing, the film deals with conflicting opinions about superstition, where real souls are at stake. Fisher also moved away from direct horror at this time and directed some science fiction films including *The Earth Dies Screaming* (1964), *Island Of Terror* (1966) and *The Night Of The Big Heat* (1967).

The Mummy (1959)

Dir: Terence Fisher. St: Christopher Lee, Peter Cushing

1895: Gammy-legged archaeologist John Banning is doing his bit for inter-cultural relations by desecrating the Tomb of Ananka and hotfooting it back to Blighty with a ton of ancient Egyptian swag. Three years later, John is set to marry Isobel when his father is strangled by a mummified corpse, currently adopting a none-too-convincing butler disguise at the home of Mehetmet Bey. The bandaged one is in fact dallying priest Kharis, entombed for his blasphemous resurrection attempts on the Princess Ananka, who just happens to bear an uncanny resemblance to John's dishy fiancée.

Hammer's plundering of Universal's back catalogue arrived at *The Mummy* in their most similar remake. Even the scenes where the Mummy, spurred on by Bey, exacts his revenge, retains a distinctly Thirties feel. Perhaps this is partly due to Hammer obtaining rights from Universal, Lee's make-up is almost identical to Karloff's but paradoxically less frightening in colour. Even if the mummy's vengeance is a touch anaemic, Lee's entrances certainly aren't, rising from a murky swamp his impossibly tall figure and unblinking eyes dominate the moonlit skyline. Being dead and musty gives Fisher ample opportunity to show the futile attempts at holding back this juggernaut of destruction - shotgun blasts spray chunks of rotten bandage around and he is even impaled (very convincingly) by a spear to no detrimental effect. The climax is pure pulp as the shambling lover holds his unconscious lookalike bride in his tattered arms, heading for the swamp's murky recesses. Fisher makes good use of the sumptuous Victorian sets (although you'll be seeing virtually every element in later Hammer period pieces) and even manages some fairly convincing Egyptian flashbacks.

The Curse Of The Werewolf (1960)

Dir: Terence Fisher St: Oliver Reed

Leon's got a thing about goats. He likes nothing better than to rip their throats out and savour the flavour. But there is a very good reason for his unorthodox lunar activities, he's a werewolf - "a body with a soul and spirit that are still at war." There are only two cures - love or a silver bullet. Naturally, the latter option is a touch drastic, which is why you'll be glad to know he goes all droopy-eyed over Christina Fernando while working with a wino Brit at the Fernando vineyard. Better still, Christina's got the hots for the hairy goat muncher too, but she's promised to another. They're classes apart and the full moon makes prospects of wedding bells far less likely than death tolls.

Werewolves have always been connected with fears of unbridled sexuality and loss of control, considered to be unholy because of their inability to curtail their base primal instincts. The beast also works as abnormal from other angles - traditionally the werewolf is male and yet suffers the same cyclic hormonal anguish as the female, emphasising the fertility aspect of menstruation by mocking it. Fisher's film manages to tackle the sexuality of werewolf myths in a shockingly frank manner for the time, showing the origin of the werewolf in more detail than its actual life. He is an "affront to God" by being born on Christmas Day, yet is christened Leon, the reverse of Noel. He doesn't stand a chance. Leon's conception is melodramatic in the extreme; his mad beggar father, rotting in the dungeons of the Marquis, rapes the mute servant girl when she is thrown to him for refusing the Marquis' advances. She savagely beats the Marquis to death on his chessboard, escaping only to die giving birth to Leon. His adopted family are kind but know of Leon's predatory moonlighting, barring his room at that difficult time of the month. It is well over halfway into the film before Reed makes his entrance.

This is a prestige production from Hammer - the village sets, including the impressive bell tower, are superbly realised and the sweep of the narrative placed real strains on the coffers. But it was worth it. Despite being set in Spain and based on folk tales, *Curse Of The Werewolf* is resolutely Victorian in its tone. It was deemed far too dark and much of the sexual and violent content was trimmed to make it acceptable as an X-rated film at the time but has subsequently been restored to its original glory.

Dracula: Prince Of Darkness (1965)

Dir: Terence Fisher St: Christopher Lee, Barbara Shelley

Two English couples on a tour of Europe are warned by Father Shandor that they shouldn't visit Carlsbad's castle. Do they listen? Of course not. Arriving at the castle, Alan is hoisted over Dracula's ashes and his throat slit reviving the Count. Helen is subsequently bitten and turns naughty nosferatu. Charles and Diana escape to find sanctuary at Shandor's monastery, but don't realise that fly-crunching resident Ludwig is more than just a little strange...

Christopher Lee returned to his most famous role, once again dominating the screen. The whole film is a tease from start to finish, Dracula not appearing until well into the running time, but this is deliberate. British to the hilt, the trappings of a horror film are used to depict the effects (albeit allegorically) of extra-marital liaisons and repressed sexuality. Helen is a frump with an annoying husband, but when freed from the restraints of her relationship and heaving in a negligee for her demonic lover, she positively glows. Of course such indiscretions warrant a phallic staking, but it was one helluva fling. Diana comes close to succumbing to her desires - the commanding Count wordlessly orders her to fling her crucifix away and tears open his shirt, offering the malevolent blood blossoming from his razor-sharp nail.

Where Fisher's original *The Horror Of Dracula* made good use of pacing, with a thrilling chase combined with comic relief, *Dracula Prince Of Darkness* generally uses characterisation to drive the narrative. Father Shandor is a classic eccentric, raucous and rude. He declares that warming his posterior by the fire in public to be "one of the few pleasures left in life" and quaffs wine with gusto. In contrast, Dracula's butler Clove has the driest wit imaginable - "Is your master indisposed?" asks Charles, "No, he's dead." With such an eclectic bunch of individuals, Fisher can do no wrong.

Visually stunning, the use of Technicolor enhances the period feel and the melodrama, and the transformation of his castle by alteration in lighting alone is astonishing. Totally dissimilar to the original (and sadly lacking Peter Cushing), this is nevertheless another fine addition to Hammer's *Dracula* series.

George A Romero (1940-)

Film production in America may be centred on Los Angeles or New York but there are film-makers who resolutely stick to home turf - John Waters keeps the flag flying for Baltimore and George A Romero is Pittsburgh's most famous director. Romero's rise to fame came with his feature film debut, an ultra-low budget highly-imaginative feature that shocked cinema audiences: *Night Of The Living Dead* (1968). Romero's style was radical – looking at social issues in the context of grim entertainment. *Jack's Wife* (aka *Season Of The Witch,* 1973) viewed the frustrations of domestically bound women by depicting a bored housewife dabbling with the occult. *The Crazies* (1973) placed the horror of *Night Of The Living Dead* into a more socially obvious context, putting a town under a brutal militaristic regime, ostensibly to curtail the spread of a virus that causes people to become 'crazies.' It becomes clear that not only were the government aware of the problem, they probably instigated it. The power of faceless white-suited storm troopers massacring families for the common good is unshakeable. It would be with *Martin* that he would make his true masterpiece and also with the second zombie film *Dawn Of The Dead* that he would finally merge consumerist critique with visceral horror. After these dizzy heights it would be difficult to please everyone.

Creepshow (1982) is perhaps his least understood film, focusing on the comic rather than nasty gore, but really it is no great departure. Using his obvious love of EC horror comics, this anthology takes its tales from stories in the non-existent comic *Creepshow* as written by Stephen King. King plays a farmer who turns into a giant vegetable and blows his own head off with a shotgun (don't ask). Other tales concern: a grumpy old bloke back from the dead (revived with spilt whiskey he croaks "I want my birthday cake" before each kill); a gurgly couple back from their watery grave to take revenge on Leslie Nielson; Adrienne Barbeau as an incredibly bitchy bitch who becomes food for a crated monster; and some nasty cockroach business with a man obsessed by cleanliness. Shot with extreme angles and exceptionally lurid primary colours, the final frames of each story fade to a comic book, complete with speech bubbles.

Day Of The Dead (1985), the third 'dead' film, saw the humans very much on the retreat, hiding in bunkers. In many respects this is another anti-militarist piece, with the zombies portrayed as the misunderstood mass, scientists even attempting to condition them. Despite the impressive special effects, there is a sense that Romero is pulling the reins on the gleeful splatter of his earlier films, preferring to comment on the breakdown of humanity.

Monkey Shines: An Experiment In Terror (1988) takes a reasonable principle (monkeys to help injured or disabled people) which turns faintly ludicrous by having a jealous serial killer monkey running amok. Surprisingly the film remains restrained in graphic gore and high on tension, managing to ride above the dubious premise with a solid cast and atmospheric soundtrack. *Two Evil Eyes* (1989) was a joint effort with Dario Argento (c.f.) based upon short stories by Edgar Allen Poe while *The Dark Half* (1993) saw him return to Stephen King territory.

Romero's contribution to the horror genre is immense, but like Argento he is influential rather than vastly successful. His ability to place supernatural horror in a wider socio-political context marks him as one of the more important genre directors.

Night Of The Living Dead (1968)

Dir: George A Romero St: Duane Jones, Judith O'Dea

A ramshackle group of people defend themselves from attacks by the reanimated dead in a backwater house, whose previous occupants have provided fleshy sustenance for the shambling cadavers.

What is so remarkable about this debut film isn't so much the oft-touted level of viscera but the fact that it's well made, intelligent and unremittingly bleak. People expect to be scared when watching a horror film - it is part of the fun - but *Night Of The Living Dead* shocked with its barbarity and lack of hope or even understanding. The use of black and white photography (a necessity of the restrictive budget) enhanced the horror - the format has always seemed more real or documentary anyway. Socially, the film could not have happened at a more opportune time - many have attributed its success to America's increasing inability to cope with the Vietnam war and there is also resonance regarding the casting of a strong black lead. This is not to say the film is entirely social commentary - there are moments of unnerving terror including the shocking sight of a recently deceased little girl stabbing her mother with a trowel. The opening cemetery sequence is straight out of the EC horror comics from which Romero derives so much of his visual inspiration. The heroine shatters all filmic expectations by spending much of the remaining time in a virtually catatonic state of shock. Corpses are found on the staircase, decomposing, half-eaten and the attempt to escape in a pick-up truck goes disastrously awry - it crashes and burns, the zombies eating the tepid remains. This last scene is so real it still shocks - Romero had his extras wolf down offal and assorted nasty bits to get the realism his budget could not afford.

Interestingly the funding of the film meant that to retain some copyright control on his creation Romero had to remake the film with most of the original crew. The 'All New' *Night Of The Living Dead* was directed by effects man Tom Savini, produced by Romero and in full bloody colour but lacks the gritty documentary punch of the original.

Martin (1977)

Dir: George A Romero St: John Amplas, Lincoln Maazel, Christine Forrest, Tom Savini

Martin is a troubled lad, cursed by visions of his past he sedates women, rapes them and drinks their blood. Cuda, his religious cousin, is duty-bound to look after the boy, decking the house with garlic and crucifixes. But is Martin a vampire or a delusional serial killer? Can he find love in the arms of a waking woman? And is his need to air his problems on a cheesy radio show a cry for understanding or a plea to be caught?

It was inevitable that Romero would be convinced to make a vampire film, but naturally *Martin* is quite unlike any other within the genre. This is a low-budget production – gritty and realistic, yet reluctant to provide definitive solutions - even by the film's close we are still unsure whether Martin is a vampire. Murder is a messy and protracted affair: Martin calms his victims before the sedative takes effect, he has to try several times with his razor to obtain a sufficient blood flow to quench his thirst, and the cleaning-up can take as long as the preparation - he fakes the deaths as suicides. He is meticulous, his crimes calculated and protracted, the sedative-filled syringes, held in his mouth like surrogate fangs, are chilling. Yet despite this, he still retains audience sympathy - his boyish looks and cries for help on the radio mean we want him to escape as much as we don't want him to kill. Cuda appears to be the real perpetrator, filling Martin's head with threats and curses and wasting no opportunity to abuse the boy. He even hires an exorcist to cast the demon from Martin. Black and white flashbacks provide Martin's dreampoint prior to periods of stress or elation, which compound the uncertainty. A classic film in every sense, it can be read on multiple levels, each subsequent viewing revealing more.

Dawn Of The Dead (1979)

Dir: George A Romero St: David Emge, Ken Foree, Gaylen Ross

When there's no more room in Hell the dead shall walk the earth. Hordes of hungry zombies roam the country, hide in basements and hang around apartments. Slow, lumbering but focused, these muscle-munching ex-people can only be stopped by a short, sharp, shot in the head. Four desperate people dream of escaping, but find themselves setting up home in a shopping mall, a fragile calm in the eye of the storm.

Financed for a pitifully small budget, especially considering the massive amount of make-up effects work, *Dawn Of The Dead* remains the ultimate zombie epic. Teaming up with Italian supremo Argento (c.f.) this is Romero's show (he wrote, directed and edited) but benefits hugely from Argento's production/distribution muscle and the music of Goblin. Even before we reach the central shopping mall, we've had the opportunity to witness a catalogue of atrocities - a basement full of zombies being annihilated by hit squads, two undead children sprayed with machine-gun fire, a helicopter blade scalping and rowdy rednecks culling zombies as a family sport. Inside the mall, our heroes begin mopping up the resident living dead and setting up home. There is a great deal of humour in these scenes, which goes a considerable way to offsetting the endless parade of carnage. We see zombies on ice, struggling on escalators and in one (perhaps too silly) scene, zombies on the receiving end of extra-gloppy custard pies. The scale of the slaughter is quite phenomenal, hundreds of Romero fans became extras, putting themselves through make-up purgatory for the privilege of being dispatched on-camera. Savini's work ranges from entrails-spilling disembowelments to lorry squashes and plenty of stringy-gored cannibalism. Many have commented on the film's approach to consumerism and the critique of capitalist values, citing the zombies' latent memories of what was important in their lives as an indictment of self-centred mall culture. Really the film's attack is more critical than even this would suggest, the main four protagonists may well wish to rid themselves of the zombie burden and head for a utopian Caribbean island but once they discover the comfort of limitless consumer appliances, they become as lazy and brainwashed as the zombies. They may well be disgruntled by the vulgar impositions of the motorcycle raiders (led by Tom Savini) but have no more right to be there than anyone else. Stacks of inferior (and occasionally far more graphic) clones were rushed out to cash in on the film's international success - Lucio Fulci's notorious *Zombie Flesh Eaters* was even marketed as *Zombi 2* in some quarters to cash in on *Dawn Of The Dead*'s continental title.

Dario Argento (1940-)

Italian cinema has given us so many movers in the horror field that it is difficult to select just one as a representative, but Dario Argento is perhaps a good choice because he reflects everything that people both love and hate about Italian horror. He is an accomplished visual stylist, drenching his canvas with intense colours and employing a dazzling array of expressive, expensive and innovative camera movements. Characterisation is secondary to the overall operatic grandeur of the whole. This is not an isolated style - much of his vision has its gestation in the world of art (particularly Delveaux and Bosch) and in other prime movers of the Italian horror film. Riccardo Freda and Mario Bava are obvious predecessors - Argento shares their love of sumptuous non-realist art decoration and stylistic excess. In particular Bava's *Blood And Black Lace* appears to hold a tight fascination with him due to its giallo origins. Giallo are pulp crime novels (originally published on yellow stocked paper) with often lurid depiction of crimes and murder. Immensely popular but frowned upon, they were ideal material for film.

Argento's first jobs in the industry were as scriptwriter on numerous projects in virtually every conceivable genre. In westerns alone this ranged from the pulpy delirium of *Five Man Army* (1969) to the internationally acclaimed Leone classic *Once Upon A Time In The West* which he co-wrote with Bernardo Bertolucci and Leone (although only credited as Story by). His first film as director, *The Bird With The Crystal Plumage* (1970 - *L'uccello Dalle Piume Di Cristallo*), features a number of women terrorised and stabbed by a black-gloved figure in a raincoat, opening with an audacious sequence where the hero, Sam, is trapped between two glass doors and is forced to watch as a terrified Monica is brutally stabbed in front of him. Argento's murderers almost always wear black gloves to disguise their identity and also, quite worryingly, give him the opportunity to do all the POV stabbing you see himself! *Cat O' Nine Tails* (1971 - *Il Gatto A Nove Code*) follows a similar thematic thread, but ditches any linear coherence in a convoluted plot about genetic research into criminal behaviour and its relation to a killer at large. *Four Flies On Grey Velvet* (1972 - *Quattro Mosche Di Velluto Grigio*), bears all the hallmarks of a good giallo - impossible to guess the murderer, extreme violence and highly convoluted plot. The title derives from the premise that the last thing a person sees before death is indelibly recorded on their retina, in this case the titular insects and their proximity to unfashionably coloured fabric. *Deep Red* (1976 - *Profondo Rosso*, confusingly titled *Suspiria 2* elsewhere) is the pinnacle of the whole giallo genre and a blueprint for Argento's subsequent work. Freed of the shackles of reality, *Suspiria* (1977) marked the start of The Three Mothers trilogy (although the third remains unmade), a delirious and hallucinogenic horror set in a girls' school. *Inferno* (1980) moved the action to New York with a virtually non-stop barrage of hypnotic colouring. In *Tenebrae* (1982 also unwisely monikered *Unsane* in a butchered US print) another writer, Peter Neale, is promoting his crime novel, the pages of which have been found stuffed in the mouth of a girl hacked to death with a razor. Argento ditches extreme colours for something a touch more antiseptic but the strong transference of guilt and some intense flashbacks pull this one back in line. Sadly the same cannot be said of *Creepers* (1985 - *Phenomena*), a misguided return to flies with an embarrassed wheelchair-bound Donald Pleasence spending a great deal of time trying to hide behind a maggot-ridden head. Far better is *Opera* (1987) which could quite easily be the title of any of his films but here it provides the setting as well as the accentuated hyper-realist tone. Again Argento's eye for the visual beauty of violence and the mechanics of the film-making process are the raison d'être of the piece with the highlight being an incredibly tense sequence where Mira (Daria Nicolodi) is looking through a keyhole only to be shot through the eye in a way both shocking and strangely ethereal. *Two Evil Eyes* (1990 - co-directed with George A Romero c.f.) is a passable Edgar Allen Poe film with Argento directing *The Black Cat* section. However the consternation over *The Stendahl Syndrome* (1997) made up for it. Argento's decision to cast his own daughter Asia in the film was not greeted with cries of nepotism, but incomprehension and fury because her character suffers the attention of a serial rapist. Despite some impressive camera tracking and, mainly blue, lighting it is not as aesthetically distancing as his best work, yet retains some of the coldness.

Argento's films, despite their debts to Hitchcock and Bava, are unremitting in their personal vision. He doesn't follow fashion but continues, albeit sporadically these days, to make films that favour aesthetics over realism. His role as producer has helped launch the careers of, in particular, two other directors - Lamberto Bava (son of Mario and maker of, among others, the gloriously over-the-top splatterfest *Demons*) and Michele Soavi (*Stagefright*, *The Sect* and *The Church*).

Deep Red (1976)

Dir: Dario Argento St: David Hemming

Marc and Carlo are jazz pianists. Marc's the bourgeois womaniser, Carlo the drunken proletariat homosexual. One night, while Marc is trying to sober up his friend he is witness to the climax of a particularly bloody killing. Soon he is embroiled in a maze of murder and intrigue, aided and occasionally hindered by arm-wrestling seductress journalist Gianna.

Deep Red is a transition from the crime pulp origins of Argento's early work to the visual experimentation and aesthetic overkill of his later films. To this end the body count is relatively modest but the intensity and attention to set detail overwhelm the proceedings. Despite its apparent basis in the 'real world' of Agatha Christie-style murders, the air of the paranormal is rife - the lecture on the telepathic power of insects and children, the occult leaning of Helga's wall paintings, the ghost house and disturbed child's drawings. Together they create a disjointed other-worldliness that is exploited by occasionally jarring camerawork. Argento's world is one of psychological manifestation and symbology; the murderer is revealed to the viewer using objects - blood red twine dolls, marbles and an assortment of knives blown up to full screen size. The murders are protracted, preceded by unbearable tension and voyeuristically subjective camerawork and then emblazoned in a raucous cacophony of intense music. Death is never trivial in Argento's films and takes on a beauty of its own, the camera cutting into the wound, exploiting the privileged position that even the most demanding voyeur would find hard to achieve. The identity of the murderer is kept secret not just because it's a mystery, but because in some sense the viewer is the murderer. This is established during the opening credits, with a children's rhyme playing over the silhouette of a stabbing - every time we hear the tune, like the murderer, we not only anticipate death (as the victim) but demand it (as the perpetrator). Flamboyant, loud and audacious both visually and aurally, *Deep Red* is so much the work of an auteur it is difficult to see who is meant to be watching this. Far too violent for the art crowd, and far too arty and formalised for everyone else, this is another slice of visceral chic.

Suspiria (1977)

Dir: Dario Argento St: Jessica Harper

"Do you know anything about witches?" Suzy's enrolment at a top dance academy gets off to a bad start as the first pupil she encounters is not only confused, but has very little time to live. Suzy's stay on campus seems doomed to failure. With her health deteriorating, maggots raining from the ceiling and the teachers appearing to leave every night (their footsteps going the wrong way), maybe there's something connected with the academy's past - not just a school for dance but of the occult as well.

The words subtle and realistic are not in *Suspiria*'s vocabulary. From the start, Argento immerses the viewer in a strange, disturbing and vicious world. In one of the most intensely meticulous murder sequences ever, a girl peers out of the yellow room into the blue darkness beyond. Two eyes stare back, a hand smashes the window and forces her head against the pane until it shatters. She is then pursued and stabbed repeatedly, the camera cutting so close as to see the knife pierce her still beating heart before she's bound with twine and dumped onto a glass ceiling. The ceiling cracks, her body falls and is jerked into hanging position inches from the floor. The remnants of the ornate glasswork have, meanwhile, found their way into the head of a passing student who is impaled to the floor like an etymologist's first display attempt. The sustained violence of the scene with its astonishing brutality and ear-bursting volume, means Argento doesn't need to bombard us with further brutalities for a substantial time and can get along with the mystery at hand. The powerful use of strong coloured lighting gives the Academy a magical feel - we know that the place is evil without the murders. *Suspiria* is about mood, style and execution; coherence and plausible dialogue are secondary.

Argento's detractors often point to *Suspiria* as a basis for repeated accusations of violence and bias against women and the disabled (*Deep Red* is often cited as homophobic too). It is difficult to deny this but there is also a sense in which they have missed the point. Argento's cinema is entirely about image. It is not factual, it is not realistic and does not campaign hatred or violence to any group. Unlike the more distasteful slasher movies, these do not gloat about violence and empower the viewer to become the violator, but are instead about the aesthetics of violence and the relationship between the voyeur and the crime. When the Academy's secrets are finally revealed we are really none the wiser; the process of reaching the conclusion is far more important than the revelations themselves. *Suspiria*'s combination of tension, graphic violence and unrepentant soundtrack makes for intoxicating viewing.

Inferno (1980)

Dir: Dario Argento

Rose is becoming obsessed with threes; 'Three Mothers,' three keys and three buildings designed by disappearing alchemist architect Varelli. Her brother Mark, a musicologist in Rome, gets an urgent call to see her but too late - she becomes another victim in a line of savage murders that seem to follow Mark like a trail of smoke to a cigarette. But what has this to do with the mothers of sighs, tears and darkness, weird bookshop owner Kazanian or murderous cats?

Inferno represents everything that is wonderful and infuriating about Argento's oeuvre. A semi-sequel to *Suspiria* we learn a little more about the Three Mothers, but not much. Narrative cohesion isn't an absolute necessity in a horror film (Fulci's garbled *The Beyond* is in a similar, if less elegant, vein) but does help to engage the viewer to visual ideas. *Inferno*'s solid refusal to pander to audience needs for a narrative form distances the viewer, turning them into coldly detached and uninvited voyeurs rather than observers. What you are left with is a sumptuous European art film, a poem of light and sound that enthrals with its sheer audacity and operatic visual form. Every frame is splashed with lurid neon-bright colour, picking out details and emphasising space at the expense of naturalism. The only time Argento departs from this is when Rose retrieves the keys in the flooded cellar beneath the house - and this is shot in such a stylised, murky light that it is just as surreal. The set pieces are so tightly bound that they flow from one to another - Rose's underground dive kicking her way to safety on the head of a decomposing body, a savage attack by cats cut short by the shocking intervention of a tramp, eyes plucked and flaming bodies falling through glass. What sets these, and other scenes of mayhem, apart is not just the virtuoso camerawork and editing, or the graphic level of blood-letting but the emphasis on the difficulty and variety of the kill. When Rose meets her end she is pinned to a window sill and has a pane of glass shoved onto her neck, not once, but twice. All Argento's trademarks are present and correct: black-gloved killer, lizards, lifts, insects and a pounding, ear-splitting soundtrack. Visually and aurally this is nothing short of miraculous but emotionally it is at best antiseptic and at worst utterly barren.

David Cronenberg (1943-)

The fiercely individual work of David Cronenberg has divided audiences and critics alike. Despite being well respected, he tends to work on lower budget films to maintain control of his projects outside of the conservative studio system. To this end he collaborates with a core base of people with whom he can trust his often bizarre and disturbing ideas - these include composer Howard Shore, designer Carol Spier, cinematographer Peter Suschitzky and costumier Denise Cronenberg. Working mainly in his native Canada, he has been the centre of controversy over films that some people find unpalatable or even obscene. What makes his work provoke such strong reactions? He deals with uncomfortable subjects: diseases, mutations, psychological deficiencies, car crashes, sexual 'perversion.' All these subjects are uncomfortably close to home, filmed in an unflinching and clinical style. He also refuses to compromise his intellectual integrity.

You don't understand what's going on? Tough, he doesn't care. He never speaks down, patronises or provides simple solutions. His best work remains on the peripheries of modern cinema, slick, thought provoking and unremittingly 'arty' in tone.

Cronenberg began making shorts at university and continued with his first feature *Stereo,* concerning telepathy experimentation that would later provide a blueprint for *Scanners. Crimes Of The Future* similarly concerned research experimentation. Neither film is conventional - with non-synced sound, excruciating long shots and a tendency to dwell on futurist architecture, they remain fascinating cult items. His first commercially released film was *Shivers* (aka *The Parasite Murders*), and its success led to *Rabid* (1977), starring Marilyn Chambers with a carnivorous sexual organ in her armpit (seriously) that turns its victims into slobbering murdering madmen. Cronenberg's next film *The Brood* (1979) dealt with the more disturbing side of motherhood and femininity. This brood of homicidal dwarf things are children bred after medical experimentation on the mother figure, physical manifestations of internal rage. This ethic of the metaphysical realised would find its ultimate protégé in the shape of Shinya Tsukamoto but remains at heart a psychological extension of the folk lycanthrope myths and their concern with bestial sexuality.

Scanners' (1981) occasionally unfathomable plot about duelling brothers with frightening telekinetic powers is most famously remembered for the astonishing opening sequence where a newsreader's head explodes through sheer mind power. It also features some extraordinary set work including a huge hollow sculpture of a head. *Videodrome* (1982) remains contentious - a masterpiece to some, an unfocused mess to others. James Woods' character is sent to investigate Videodrome, a television station where people are taken to be sexually abused for the viewers' entertainment. What makes the film so edgy is Woods' embroilment into the Videodrome ethos eventually resulting in neither the characters nor the viewers having any idea of what is real and what is hallucination. After such an audacious work it is perhaps unsurprising that *The Dead Zone* (1983), a Stephen King adaptation starring Christopher Walken as a man fresh out of a coma discovering he has precognitive powers, was so insipid.

Following this, Cronenberg made a trilogy of unusual love stories - *The Fly, Dead Ringers* and *M. Butterfly* (1993). He also moved onto some ambitious projects, attempting to film the 'unfilmable.' William Burroughs' cult novel *Naked Lunch* (1991), a cross-cutting between biography and fiction, succeeded admirably visually but ultimately failed to emote. Then J G Ballard's *Crash* (1996) allowed the characters to wallow in their deviant sexual pleasures, Cronenberg filming wounds and scars with the touch of a pornographer, enticing the viewer to derive gratification from the mutilation of the human form. After a press furore over the eventual decision to pass the film uncut in the UK, hundreds of people went to be 'revolted' by this 'obscenity' and were merely bored. For those familiar with Cronenberg's output it was another wonderful film with a particularly hallucinatory Howard Shore score.

eXistenZ (1999) was a far less contentious affair featuring Jude Law as a man trapped (or not...) inside a living computer game that acts via an umbilical jack plug inserted in the base of the spine. Unlike *Videodrome* though, everything is explained by the film's close. Eminently watchable and a good, solid ride, it just lacks the cerebral depth of some of his other films.

At his best Cronenberg is an innovator of dark, clinical films which deal with human sexuality, disease and the mutation of physicality. Occasionally, his precision can leave the viewer as cold as the films they are watching, but overall his commitment to intellectual but unflinching horror is remarkable.

Shivers (1976)

Dir: David Cronenberg St: Paul Hampton, Lynn Lowry, Barbara Steele

Welcome to Starliner Towers, your new, safe home on Starliner Island, a world away from the bustle of the city. We have plush, clean apartments to suit everyone and our team of friendly staff will tend to all your needs, be they medical or recreational. Enjoy the security and safety that only Starliner can offer you. You can be sure that your neighbours will be people just like you - happy, regular, decent people all willing to spread their experimental parasitic venereal disease with liberal abandon and invite you into their happy, pacifist word of glassy-eyed orgies and sexual experimentation.

Shivers wasn't released into cinemas, it was unleashed. Cronenberg's first 'commercial' (if that word can be used) feature is a gleeful orgy of sexual violation and integration. Cronenberg is relentless and unflinching, a voyeur looking from the doorways of the apartment block - it's like staring in on your neighbours. Even the opening has a strong sense of shock and outrage as the mundane aspects of a couple purchasing an apartment intercuts with Dr Hobbes' savage attack on Annabelle. Annabelle is wearing schoolgirl's clothing and the doctor's intentions are anything but clear. It is only later that we find out she was a prostitute and by then he has strangled her, sliced her open, poured acid into her stomach cavity and slit his own throat. All to no avail because Nick Tudor has contracted the parasite anyway. Cronenberg filmed this queasy opening partly handheld. It's intimate and violent, implying the viewer's active engagement. Dr Hobbes' parasites were designed to replace unhealthy human organs, but his ideas took a grandiose turn for the bizarre - "man is an animal that thinks too much," he reasoned and set about instigating world peace by creating a parasite that was "a combination of aphrodisiac and venereal disease that would turn the world into one big orgy." It worked too. Before long, Nick is tending his new parasites like pets as they visibly move around his stomach area - a queasy effect that has subsequently been used many times, from *The X-Files* to *The Mummy*. By the end, his body is riddled with an impressive brood, all wiggling free from his smoking abdomen in bloody eagerness to find a host. No one is safe, regardless of age (both hobbly old pensioners and schoolchildren are up for a bit of French kissing), sexual persuasion or gender; once you've got the parasite you become a bisexual nymphomaniac. In one notorious scene (there are many, many of them) Barbara Steele has a rather intimate bath-time encounter with a creature from the plughole, thrashing around before succumbing to amorous bliss - the image is exploited to the max in the film's hysterically sleazy poster, dragging in a larger audience than the promise of an arthouse film with allusions to J G Ballard and Philip K Dick ever would. The parasites themselves are like phallic, bloody turds that leap into people's mouths and turn them into sex mad, uncontrollable but happy people. Yes they are savagely attacked but, Cronenberg seems to be saying, aren't they so much nicer now? In many ways this is a pornographic film for lovers of disease where "everything is erotic - disease is the love of two alien creatures for each other." The parasites cannot exist without their hosts, and the hosts are blissfully healthy. So it's a happy ending after all. Ahhh.

The Fly (1986)

Dir: David Cronenberg St: Jeff Goldblum, Geena Davis

Seth Brundle hates to travel - it's a motion thing - which explains why he wants to build a teleporter. After falling for journalist Veronica at a dull party he continues trials with baboons and steaks until he achieves success. Fuelled by alcohol and an unfounded concern that Veronica is ditching him for her repulsive ex-boyfriend, Seth himself enters the telepod. Unfortunately, so does a housefly resulting in genetic level splicing and he emerges Brundlefly. Now he has a disease with a purpose - half benevolent, half malevolent - but can true love run its course as he gets progressively less human and sheds more body parts?

Often dismissed by Cronenberg's admirers as his 'slight commercial film,' *The Fly* remains his most financially lucrative work. At heart it's as simple as you can get and a very emotional experience; boy meets girl, they fall in love, something comes between them. Brundle's world is so isolated it is appropriate that we rarely venture from it; set mostly in one room, this could have quite easily been a play. Goldblum is in his element as Brundle, a geeky, twitchy guy with cringeworthy sense of humour and a line in identical suits. Until he is merged with the fly, that is. Then he becomes irritable, paranoid, superfit and a marathon shag machine ("Penetration beyond the veil of the flesh"). All these changes are visible not just in the make-up but also in Goldblum's expressive mannerisms. Like most of Cronenberg's oeuvre, the disease is not seen in an entirely negative light by either the victim or the film - Seth isn't better or worse, just different. The concern lies with Brundle's development - the rapid metabolism of the fly creates bizarre side effects; he may need to walk on crutches but he can climb on the ceiling, he might deposit his body parts in The Brundle Museum of Natural History but he can leap through windows and carry people up stairs without breaking into a sweat. The damage to Veronica is entirely psychological, she is forced to shotgun her man in the head and suffers horrific visions of aborting a maggot (delivered by Cronenberg himself in a suitably sick cameo). However, the film's ultimate feelgood message is that love can thrive no matter how someone looks.

A more violent, shallow but watchable sequel *The Fly II* (Walas, 1989) was made but remains an inferior film, lacking the emotion that people wrongly assume Cronenberg is incapable of showing.

Dead Ringers (1988)

Dir: David Cronenberg St: Jeremy Irons, Jeremy Irons, Geneviève Bujold

"We make women fertile and that's all we do." Elliot and Beverly Mantle are identical twins. They are also gynaecologists. Oh, and Beverley is going mad. He's the quiet sensitive, psychotic genius while Elliot is the confident public face of their international success. They share everything, including patient Claire Niveau, an actress whose promiscuous desire for offspring triggers the brothers' descent into a downward spiral of drug addiction, insanity and eventually death.

Despite the absence of graphic bloodletting and low body count, *Dead Ringers* still manages to be Cronenberg's most disturbing film. Partly this is due to it being based on reality, but mainly because of the matter-of-fact way that he creates his tale - the morbid events are horrific enough, so he wisely stays clear of any sensationalism (except for one particularly outré dream sequence). The horror lies in the surgical treatment of women and the normality of the surgery on show. Irons gives Oscar-worthy performances as the twins, you never doubt who is whom and it's far more than Beverly wearing the fuddy-duddy jumper. The shots where the twins appear together are remarkable for being unremarkable; there is no fanfare as we casually view the two talking side by side while being tracked down a corridor.

Matters turn to the surreal when the production and costume design is given full reign; pillar-box red robes bleed against the clinical white of the surgery and, most horrible of all, bizarre surgical instruments are manufactured by an artist. These gnarled metal sculptures of surgical torture are the film's strongest image - intricate and possessing half-grasped concepts of probing and pain. Perhaps deeper is the implication that women deprived of the ability to reproduce find solace in self-abasement and degradation. Claire confesses to being "extremely promiscuous," demanding that she is "bad and needs to be punished" which, for her sins, she is; tied up with surgical appliances prior to coitus, unaware that she is the sexual plaything of both brothers. There is a sense that the links between sex and death, creation and destruction are strong, the wound a source of pleasure as well as pain. Elliot's death at the hands of his brother may be surgical but is purely sexual - he is splayed out like a dissected rat. The implications of using the very instruments of his brother's medical research to create a vagina-like cavity in his body are all too clear. He is effectively feminized and brutalised in one act. By no means a conventional film *Dead Ringers* rewards subsequent viewing because of its subtlety and depth while retaining that 'too close for comfort' edge.

Joe Dante (1946-)

Born in New Jersey, Joe Dante's unusual portfolio takes the language of conventional Hollywood film-making and turns it on its head. Often insanely surreal for mainstream pictures, Dante's best work can be viewed on many levels - either as a straight linear narrative, a subversive look at American mores, criticising consumerist desires or as a rich source of filmic in-jokes. This playfulness, using riddles, appropriated genre names and visual references make Dante's films fun to watch, like a roller-coaster and puzzle mixed together. As such he is among the first of the postmodern horror directors. His lifelong love of cartoons and (especially Fifties) science fiction/horror films permeates his work with cinephilic glee, as though he is having as much fun creating and destroying his 'toys' on screen as his admirers have soaking up the finished results of his labours. Dante began his apprenticeship under Roger Corman, editing trailers before co-directing *Hollywood Boulevard* with Alan Arkin, a parody of the low-grade production company who funded the picture. This black comedic referential style would put him in good stead for his solo feature *Piranha* (1978) which is more than the *Jaws* rip-off it was initially dismissed as. Its deserved success gave Dante a bigger budget to make *The Howling* (1980), a hip deconstruction of the werewolf film. By now he had secured larger studio investment in his ideas, starting with the best part of the multi-director portmanteau film *The Twilight Zone*. Again blending a love of cartoons, violence and black humour, his segment features a boy whose family and a passing stranger have to maintain a grotesque 'happiness' if they are to remain unmolested by the phantasmagorical manifestations of cartoon characters that police the heavily distorted house. Dante's first smash followed - the deeply irresponsible anarcho-horror-comedy *Gremlins*. Then came a stint directing segments of *Amazing Stories* and the variable B-movie spoof *Amazon Women On The Moon* (1987).

Explorers (1985) is an amiable tale of a pug-ugly alien who befriends an all-American boy. What's more, the alien can even speak English, but its only comprehension comes from television shows whose ever-happy lines he spurts out to the point of meaningless garbage. A better example of the flip side of Spielberg's world is hard to imagine. Dante is just as cruel but seems to revel in the chaos as much as his hero Chuck Jones (a regular cameo star of many of his films). *InnerSpace* (1987) was a visually impressive but fairly lacklustre reworking of *Fantastic Voyage* (1966) and *The 'burbs* (1988) took a twisted look at peculiar neighbours. *Matinee* (1993) features John Goodman as a thinly-disguised version of low-budget filmmaker William Castle, promoting his cheesy horror films like a carnival event, full of tacky gimmicks and tricks. It's a nostalgic look at one of America's most eccentric film businessmen as Goodman goes about financing, making and hawking his latest brainchild *Mant!* "Half man, half ant, all terror." Dante's dedication to the B-movie process went as far as to make *Mant* itself, used in part of the film. If it had been shot in Emergo it would have been perfect. After more TV work including *Eerie, Indiana*, Dante returned to the big screen with *Small Soldiers* (1998), reverting to the consumerist pastiche of *Gremlins*, which simultaneously entertains with its over-the-top violence and asides to American militarism.

Piranha (1978)

Dir: Joe Dante St: Heather Menzies, Brad Dillman, Barbara Steele, Paul Bartel

Those military types genetically manufactured an all-water, super-savage, fast-breeding breed of piranha in order to win the Vietnam war. But before they could let loose Operation Razorteeth's ferocious fishies, the conflict ended leaving them nothing to eat but the odd straying skinny dipper. Dizzy investigator Maggie is hunting for two such errant youngsters but her reckless investigation unwittingly unleashes the snappy critters into the river. With a summer camp packed full of kids downstream, it's only a matter of time before the nasty nippers gnaw at the noisy nippers.

John Sayles' witty script has its tongue wedged as far in its cheek as a piranha's oversized jaw. Although comparisons with *Jaws* are inevitable, *Piranha* stands out amongst the multitude of pretenders by its brazen disregard for taste, playful exuberance and ante-upping manoeuvres on every aspect of Spielberg's earnest horror film. *Jaws* has a dead skinny dipper at the start? *Piranha* has two. *Jaws* has one carnivorous fish? *Piranha* has a school of 'em. A kid on an inflatable gets it? A whole camp full of little darlings get it. Instead of an inept vote-conscious mayor, we have the camp (in more ways than one) leader played with gusto by cult director Paul Bartel (*Eating Raoul, Death Race 2000*) who rules his adopted mob with incredulous stupidity. Similarly the army deal with the matter in as over-the-top way they can, by poisoning the water - "We'll just pollute the bastards to death."

Dante films his killers with a frenetic pace and almost abstract intensity. Partly this disguises the fact that they are clearly puppets but it adds a great deal of vigour to the proceedings, masking the action with gallons of blood and cutting swiftly between shots. Being small in size but large in number the resultant injuries are horrific, no chewed-off limbs but lots of gnawed gaping wounds. Everything escalates towards the conclusion, each attack multiplying in on-screen ferocity to keep the audience's attention. The level of violence is high and often grizzly but it remains in essence cartoon, the premise itself is daft enough to support this. The irony of it is that *Piranha* is gorier, tighter, less pompous and funnier than *Jaws* and doesn't leave you freaking out at the concept of swimming.

Successful enough to spawn a sequel, *Piranhas II: The Flying Killers* is more stupid than even the title suggests with winged piranhas massacring a yuppie barbecue. Directed by James Cameron the film contains some similar underwater camerawork to his blockbuster *Titanic*.

The Howling (1980)

Dir: Joe Dante St: Dee Wallace, Patrick MacNee, Dennis Dugan, John Carradine, Slim Pickens

Top psychiatrist Dr Waggner, her employers and hubby Bill all agree that TV journalist Karen White should take a break. After all, she has come perilously close to being mutilated by Eddie the Mangler. What better place for respite than the good doctor's Colony in the country? Actually there are lots of better places - the residents are bonkers, Marsha is a nymphomaniac with an eye for Bill, and there's a cabin in the woods decked out with animal remains. Good thing the place isn't crawling with lycanthropes then...

It's typical: you wait ages for a decent werewolf film to turn up (emphasis on decent, *Werewolf Of Washington* and *The Beast Must Die* do not count) and then two come along at once. Although oft compared to *An American Werewolf In London* (1981) the two are fundamentally different. Landis' finest hour is single focused, single werewolved, quadruped, expensive and very funny while Dante's is (relatively) cheap, ambitious, multi-wolved, bipedal and a lot more disturbing. Within the space of a commercial exploitation film, Dante has produced an eye-catching critique of the watching process. Rather than centre on the obvious aspects of horror film's fascination with voyeurism, *The Howling* confronts the ethics of the entire viewing experience by bombarding the screen with images of filming and its consequences. The flicker of the porno film with Karen's reaction flashed back on a camera lens pointing at her, Karen photographing pictures at the cabin while she herself is framed by a mirror and the opening of video static all go towards questioning the nature of watching. Then there are all manner of references to wolves in the media; the characters, notably Terry Fisher and Fred Francis, have names that affectionately refer to werewolf film directors while the fully converted lycanthrope is bipedal in the manner of that shown in the cartoon of the *Three Pigs* (which plays in the background along with more orthodox wolf fare). These transformations start out half-seen but impressive (as when Marsha and Bill change during coitus) and escalate to full-on effects work, all bubbling skin, ripping nails and protruding jaws. These are ferocious beasts; biting mid-jump, slashing deep, severed arms shimmer back into their human form, Eddie ejects a bullet from his head like he's squeezing a spot, and the pack relish their superiority. Indeed they are superior to the point of arrogance - they exhibit flagrant disbelief that anyone would have the foresight to pre-pack silver bullets (conveniently purchased from a New York esoteria emporium). *The Howling* delivers everything an exploitation horror film should.

Gremlins (1984)

Dir: Joe Dante St: Phoebe Cates, Hoyt Axton, Zach Galligan, Scott Bradly

When Rand Peltzer buys a mogwai named Gizmo for his son Billy, he is warned there are three rules that he must obey: keep it out of the light, don't let it get wet and most importantly never, ever feed it after midnight. Naturally, Gizmo does accidentally have water spilled on him and five furry new Gizmos spring from his back. Not so bad then. But these new mogwai are very naughty, trick Billy into feeding them after midnight and transform into Gremlins. Oops!

Gremlins is a great film - funny, silly and sick. It paves the way for the Nineties horror film, with lots of emphasis of the rules, a good deal of foreshadowing and plenty of references to other films. Gizmo is the ultimate bundle of fun, years before Japanese cartoons entered Western culture - he's all big wide eyes, little button nose and endearing squeaks. The gremlins though are a sharp contrast - scaly skin, pointy teeth and evil cackles as they set about causing chaos. Because the film was produced by Spielberg, the extra budget gave Dante the clout to have armies of homicidal pets run amok in middle America. And what fun they have - they are completely anarchic, so their executions are justifiably outrageous, but fun, particularly those at the hands of Billy's mum, who knocks one into a food processor and splats another in the microwave. Dante's references here all relate to Christmas – Gizmo is a present, Billy's girlfriend Kate hates the festive season because her father was found dead in their chimney dressed like Santa Claus and there are nods to festive films such as Capra's *It's A Wonderful Life,* and the wonderful *Wizard Of Oz*. The film's combination of splatter and cute has endeared it to as many people as were repulsed by it, or dismissed it as being childish. A belated sequel *Gremlins 2: The New Batch* was also directed by Dante and is just as much fun - think muppets with gore.

Wes Craven (1949-)

The terms Wes Craven and horror are synonymous. For almost thirty years, Craven has been scaring mainstream audiences and has been responsible for creating a number of familiar horror icons. Although his reputation is that of shockmaster, his films are actually intelligent. There are certain themes that run throughout most of his work - teenagers coming to terms with growing up, alongside parental conflicts or guilt transference. Dreams play an important role - the merging of fantasy with reality not only provides an opportunity to produce some stunning and surreal imagery, but acts as a useful device to create scares or shocks. Starting his career as an editor, Craven's first opportunity to direct came from the Sean Cunningham-produced *Last House On The Left* (1972). This vicious exploitation revenge movie where a gang of rapist murderers are themselves tortured when a house they visit happens to be home to their victim's parents is a modern-day version of Bergman's *The Virgin Spring* (1959). It remains banned in the UK and routinely condemned elsewhere. Craven's next project was the brutal *The Hills Have Eyes* (1977) concerning a family of campers at the top of the menu when they bump into a group of cannibals. The tension throughout is high, particularly a scene involving a gun being shoved into a mouth and the trigger being slllloooowwly pulled. After spending some time working in TV, Craven directed *Deadly Blessing* (1981) featuring a religious sect pursuing a woman. It had some nice dream imagery, Sharon Stone and little else. *The Hills Have Eyes II* (1985) couldn't match its predecessor's tense nastiness but revived 'that bald bloke' for another creepy outing. *Swamp Thing* (1982) based on the DC comic was fun, silly and had its tongue firmly in its cheek, although it was at times surprisingly moving. Adrienne Barbeau was the woman for whom a giant mutant vegetable creature (once a scientist) would fall in love. It was in 1984 that he consolidated his position as a mainstream horror director with the genuinely scary *A Nightmare On Elm Street* starring serial slayer Freddy Krueger. Its timing and success ensured that sequels would follow, and although Craven himself had very little input to the subsequent films (save writing the only passable entry in Part Three), follow they did. Just when Freddy had really seemed to have breathed his last, Craven returned to him in 1994 with *Wes Craven's New Nightmare*, a knowing self-referential nod to the series, that characterised many horror films of the mid to late Nineties. After the first *Elm Street*, his movies ranged from the weird and bizarre to rather trite mainstream - it was never easy to predict how the next one would turn out. *Deadly Friend* (1986), a typical teen *Weird Science*-esque shocker about a dead girl being given a robot's brain, was suitably brainless. *The Serpent And The Rainbow* (1987) took Bill Pullman to Haiti, where he would search for a drug used by voodoo priests and encounter all sorts of creepy-crawlies and weird dreams. The utterly barmy *Shocker* (1989) featured a serial killer who, as a result of his electrocution, could travel through televisions and electrical wiring, whilst maintaining a psychic link with a kid. Incongruous, occasionally very nasty it bounces like a mad thing from the tired prison horrors it pastiches to slapstick scatological humour derived in part from Keaton's *Sherlock Jnr* (1924). *The People Under The Stairs* was a quirky and paranoid little number while *Vampire In Brooklyn* (1995) proved popular due to the appearance of Eddie Murphy as a vampire seeking his true love. With a preposterous script, and a few sick moments, this is one that relies on the comedy and is better than expected.

The third era of Craven's career began when he teamed up with script-writer Kevin Williamson in the Nineties. *Scream* launched a new series of horrors and created a template for many current postmodern horror films. The combination of Williamson's sassy and streetwise scripting with Craven's considerable experience creating scares was an unmitigated success. Two sequels followed with Craven making an unexpected diversion into the bitter-sweet drama territory with *Music Of The Heart* (1999).

Despite his reputation as a modern master of horror, Craven's films usually have an air of difference about them that has proven influential on his peers. Even as producer on films like *Wishmaster*, his name is a 'stamp of approval' on many video covers.

A Nightmare On Elm Street (1984)

Dir: Wes Craven St: Johnny Depp, Ronnee Blakley, Nick Corri, Robert Englund

A group of friends are having nightmares, really terrifying ones that seem to have a warped and twisted reality. Not long after, Tina and Rod are killed in their sleep. Nancy begins to realise that dreams can come true. It then becomes horribly clear that she's up against child murderer Freddy Krueger, who was burnt to death by vigilante parents some years before.

A Nightmare On Elm Street remains a defining point in Eighties horror films; Freddy's appeal having much to do with the cut of his costume - the dirty sweater, the hat and, of course, the razor-endowed glove. Freddy is a sadist and a child killer, but most importantly he is not tangible – he does not exist in the real world and therefore seems unassailable. Craven combines the inevitability of succumbing to sleep with the savagery of the serial slayer. It's an outstanding move, the victims must sleep eventually (an update on *Invasion Of The Body Snatchers*), and the film can focus and play upon on the blurring between reality and dreamtime, a theme that Craven uses regularly. The dream sequences make the whole film one extended set piece, phasing in and out of alternative realities - Nancy following a trail of blood in the wake of her body-bagged friend, Glen sucked into his bed only to be ejected as a volcanic eruption of gore, Freddy's abnormally wide arms sparking the walls with his blades and the terrifying sequence in the bath as Nancy drifts into sleep and the glove emerges through the bubbles to drag her down. Craven never lets go - spooky kid's rhymes, half-grasped horrors and stilted whispers of unspeakable atrocities. Iconic and influential, it spawned more imitators and sequels than were strictly necessary.

The People Under The Stairs (1991)

Dir: Wes Craven St: Brandon Adams, Everett McGill, Wendy Robie

Poindexter's family ain't doing so good, facing eviction from their nasty landlords. The only way 'Fool' Dexter can think of raising triple rent in double quick time is to steal the money from the landlords themselves, hence adding a sense of irony to the proceedings. Trouble is, a thirteen year old burgling a house of two resolutely evil people doesn't seem like good odds and, what's more, there are creatures that live under the stairs whose idea of fast food is more human than bovine.

The US class system and prejudicial attitudes confronted allegorically as a horror film with midget cannibals and the Hurleys from *Twin Peaks* really shouldn't work, but strangely it does. Poor little Alice is kept in line by her 'mummy and daddy' who lock her in and chastise her for helping to feed the people under the stairs. Told that "bad girls go to Hell" she is the product of capitalist motivation and greed taken to its limits - she must be seen to be good despite the atrocities within the house. The people under the stairs have become the literal underclass because of their oppression but do nothing to escape their plight. It is only when they are pushed too far that they finally revolt, but by then what possible hope of humanity remains? Craven's typically surreal sense of horror is allowed full reign; a deformed arm stretching out from the skirting boards, electrified doors, Father's gimp fetish suit and a dog with a severed hand in its mouth. Because the film rarely ventures outside the walls of the house it maintains a menacing air of claustrophobia. In some respects this is actually a warped updating of Hansel and Gretel with Alice and Dexter as two children at the mercy of adults, running away through a scary urban forest. Despite not achieving commercial success, *The People Under The Stairs* is nonetheless one of Craven's most satisfying films.

Scream (1996)

Dir: Wes Craven St: Neve Campbell, Drew Barrymore, David Arquette, Courtney Cox

Sidney has been having a rough time since her mother died. Things don't get any better though when her boyfriend is thrown into jail, there's an irritating journalist hassling her and everyone she knows starts getting stalked by a mysterious masked killer.

The movie that resurrected a genre, *Scream* owes a huge debt to its predecessors from the Seventies and Eighties, but crucially doesn't compromise what made them so popular in the first place. Like *Friday The Thirteenth*'s hockey mask and Freddy's glove, the killer's billowing black cape and mask (very Munch) make for easy audience identification, and simultaneously allow the killer's identity to remain unknown until the very end. The film's a comedy and a quiz in one - genre devotee Randy lays down the rules of the horror film to the assembled throng - don't have sex, do drugs and never say "I'll be right back," just before disappearing off on his own. It never balks when it comes to the scares and the gore, so that while the revelations are as obscure as expected, the tension remains. Indeed the original cut of the film was deemed too scary, so some of the murders (notably the opening killing of Casey's eviscerated boyfriend) are trimmed, but this doesn't detract from your enjoyment - the build-ups and red herrings are always the scariest bits anyway. *Scream 2* capitalised on the 'rules of the sequel' by increasing the body count and the elaborate manner of the deaths but fortunately not decreasing the quality. The same cannot be said of the passable *Scream 3*, a sign that being self-referential can turn a film into a bore (it was not, incidentally, penned by Williamson) between some admittedly fun set pieces.

Clive Barker (1952-)

Clive Barker shot to fame with his *Books Of Blood*, a series of horror short stories and novellas notable for their attention to visceral minutia and graphic descriptions of mythical horrors. These and the publication of longer works placed him in the limelight as one of the world's premiere contemporary horror writers. But Barker is more than just a writer of stories, he has written theatre productions, scripts, is a talented (if disturbing) artist whose works often adorn his books' dustjackets and, of course, he is a film director.

Barker's first foray into the celluloid world began with the short *Salome* (1973), an amateur black and white 16mm film concerning the last days of

John the Baptist. Although cheaply shot, the influence of Jean Cocteau and Kenneth Anger is apparent. *The Forbidden* (1975) is even more avant-garde in its execution. Shot entirely in negative which further increases the hallucinatory nightmarish aspect, like its forebear it remained unseen until well after Barker had established himself as a mainstream director.

His first feature film production came with *Underworld* (1985), a tale of medical mutants cowering in their own society, fearful of the evil doctor who created them. The script was written purely for the screen but there are certainly hints of *Cabal* (*Nightbreed*) present. Next came *Rawhead Rex* (1986), adapted by Barker from his own short story concerning the awakening of a nine-foot pre-Roman beast with an insatiable appetite for flesh. Both of these films were directed by George Pavlou on pitifully low budgets and went straight to video. Unperturbed, Barker adapted his story *The Hellbound Heart* into a tight screenplay, showing that a visceral, believable horror film could be made cheaply by directing it himself. The film was *Hellraiser* and its success launched a franchise from which Barker would reap rewards.

He continued as producer on the *Hellraiser* series but a far more successful film resulted in the adaptation of his story *The Forbidden* as *Candyman* (Rose, 1992). Key to the film's success is the slow, foetid pace of the tale and the way that it remains unsettling, nasty and genuinely shocking, remaining faithful to its source. Again sequels resulted.

Nightbreed saw Barker embark on a large scale studio project but the final results were hacked by befuddled executives worried about how to market the end result. *Lord Of Illusions* similarly suffered studio hostility. Sadly he has not returned to the director's chair but continues to exert a huge influence on the media, introducing his *A To Z Of Horror* for the BBC and continuing to write. His oft-mentioned affinity with fellow British director James Whale led to his enthusiastic involvement in Bill Condon's moving film of the last days of that director's life *Gods And Monsters* (1998) as executive producer.

Barker's work is replete with religious (often pagan) symbolism and the links between pleasure and pain. The mechanics of death, mutilation and the horror process are never shied from within his work and develop a masochistic aesthetic of their own. In *Hellraiser* the Cenobites are shown "opening the doors of Heaven and Hell" to give their victim "pleasure and pain indivisible," and as a director and visionary Barker does nothing less.

Hellraiser (1987)

Dir: Clive Barker St: Andrew Robinson, Clare Higgins, Ashley Laurence

Frank's a very naughty boy, in seeking new thrills his body and soul have been ripped asunder by the decidedly unpleasant Cenobites. It's down to his lover (and wife of his brother Larry) Julia to supply him with human blood so he can reassemble his body and escape the supernatural clutches of the sadists who want his very being.

Barker's feature debut is an audacious display of extremely unpleasant imagery, executed with astonishing special effects that are at times rather too realistic for comfort. The plot is painfully basic but this is used to create a mythical inevitability. In many horror films, the act of showing the monster dissipates the terror, but Barker's depictions are so extreme they confront the viewer directly and, crucially, conceal a greater menace. When the leading Cenobite intones "We have such sights to show you" the implications are all too clear - the atrocities we have seen are paltry hors d'oeuvres to a far more substantial main course. The main drive is the boundary between sexual pleasure and pain; both Frank and Julia are consumed by their sadomasochistic desires. Their victims are complicit in their own demise, stupid sex-driven businessmen fuelled on their testosterone-charged egos. The Cenobites are hideous caricatures of fetishistic extremes, all flayed flesh, surgical implements and leather bondage gear. Julia is shot in the style of a Forties glamour star with sparkling jewellery, glistening eyes and iconographical backlighting while Frank is straight out of a Kenneth Anger film, all tattoos and gay biker styling. The lighting throughout maintains this blandness within the real world and a glossy stylisation whenever the Cenobites invade the drabness - blue rays cast through shutters, catching the dancing dust. In terms of make-up and effects work *Hellraiser* never puts a foot wrong - Frank's resurrection as a bloody skeleton emerging from a pool of viscera, the gradual muscle regeneration like a gory reversal of Whale's *Invisible Man*, or the chattering teeth of the Helnwein-style Cenobite. Barker softens the blow by placing the threat in a fantasy context - Kirsty's solving of the puzzle reveals an endless corridor patrolled by a horrendous beast, while the mysterious locust-eating tramp regains the puzzle cube and transforms into a skeletal dragon. Both of these sequences are highly reminiscent of the works of Terry Gilliam, particularly *Time Bandits* and *Jabberwocky*. Likewise, there are nods to Franju in the dream sequences and asides to Polanski's *Repulsion*. *Hellraiser* plays as a very nasty moralistic fable which offers all the trappings of the genre and visceral excess to amuse and terrify the undiscerning, but with enough depth to satisfy those seeking more.

Nightbreed (1990)

Dir: Clive Barker St: David Cronenberg

Beneath the soil, beneath the corpses lies another world, Midian, where the monsters go. Boon, tortured by nightmares, is receiving psychiatric help from Dr Decker. Help in the loose sense of the word, because Decker is a brutal, masked serial killer whose self-preservation goes so far as to get Boon shot. Dead, Boon becomes Nightbreed, a resident of Midian whose people are sensitive or different from the Naturals above ground. What's below stays below, but Decker wants entrance to Midian without the pain.

Fuelled by the critical and commercial success of *Hellraiser*, Barker adapted another of his stories, *Cabal*, for the big screen. Unfortunately, despite the grotesque imagery and graphic deaths, the studio was not impressed. They wanted unambiguous and evil monsters, not complex or sympathetic ones, so they recut the picture and provided a highly misleading promotional campaign that emphasised the horror, which was subservient to the fantastical drive of the narrative. What remains may well be a poor relation to Barker's original cut (we may never know) but is not the unmitigated mess that some have levelled at it. Cronenberg's Dr Decker is clinically ruthless in his pursuit of knowledge through pain, his killer's mask a crude leather reworking of a gimp headpiece with a disfigured zip grin. He is the real 'monster' of the piece, torturing without remorse to achieve his horrendous ends. The inhabitants of Midian, no matter how horrifying they are to look at, are either misguided, confused or normally just scared and a little bit pathetic in comparison. Barker's sympathies with the underdogs appear like Browning's *Freaks* but the resonance is deeper than that. The Nightbreed actively engage in unusual, some would say revolting, practices because that is how they are - different but not intrinsically evil. Boon becomes an inspiration to the denizens of Midian, inciting them to forego their timid natures and fight for the right to be different. Midian itself is a chaotic flame-lit city, its storytale reputation its greatest defence. Again the protagonist (hero is not really a term you can use in Barker's oeuvre) becomes a pagan mythical figure by the film's open-ended close. In this respect *Nightbreed* becomes an adult fairy tale, whose basically simplistic structure disguises a rich mythical undercurrent.

Lord Of Illusions (1995)

Dir: Clive Barker St: Scott Bakula, Kevin J O'Connor, Famke Jannsen, Daniel Von Bargen

Thirteen years ago Swann banished cult leader Nix to a very deep grave, screwed a holding mask to his head and rescued a kidnapped girl called Dorothea. Now Swann is a stage illusionist and his old colleagues are being bumped off by two of Nix's fanatical disciples trying to find their master's resting place so they can resurrect him.

Like Alan Parker's *Angel Heart, Lord Of Illusions* seeks to merge film noir with supernatural horror, hence "walking the path between trickery and divinity." Barker invests all the seriousness he can muster from the outset; dead chickens, dust-blown bones, eviscerated dogs, arcane symbols and the sound of flies in the air. By declaring that there are two types of magic - illusory and genuine - the viewer is often left in doubt as to what is real and what is fake but, thanks to some brief yet vivid flashbacks, is convinced that real magic does exist. Nix's rule over his followers is so complete that they await his return for over a decade, but Butterfield and his seemingly painless companion (who only stops moving when impaled on an extremely phallic stage prop) take a more proactive role in resurrecting their beloved leader.

In some ways Barker's film is about eyes and the act of looking, as though he too is the magician manipulating his audience, daring us to challenge the validity of what we see. Nix's power seems to come from his eyes: they are the first thing to be denied him prior to incarceration (in a scene inspired by Bava's *Mask Of Satan*), eyeballs are eaten, and Dorothea hides her eyes behind her fingers but still peeps through. It is as though Barker expects his audience to do the same. Indeed, he piles on the atrocities with consummate attention to detail. Most astonishing is the resurrection of Nix, shown in a continuous shot as the camera tracks into a bullet wound and through the body where we can see the regeneration of his internal organs. The climax is a riot of surreal imagery, aided and abetted by an appropriately ominous score from ex-Goblin Simon Boswell. Unlike *Hellraiser*, in *Lord Of Illusions* the characters, whatever their faults, at least mean something to us.

Resource Materials

Books

Aurum Film Encyclopedia Horror, Ed: Phil Hardy, Aurum Press, ISBN: 1-85410-384-9 Covering the entire horror movie genre in chronological order, this is the definitive (and heavy) film review reference. Excellent coverage of some of the more obscure films and world horror cinema.

BFI Companion To Horror, Ed: Kim Newman, Cassel, ISBN: 0-304-33213-5 Covering the entire horror movie genre by subject, this is another weighty tome. It deals with the movers and themes within horror as well as key films.

Fragments Of Fear by Andy Boot, Creation Books, ISBN: 9-871592-35-6 An illustrated guide to British Horror films. If you want an in-depth guide to the wonderful worlds of Hammer, Tigon and Amicus or more info on such directors as Michael Reeves or Clive Barker, this is a super guide to all horrors British.

Censored by Tom Dewe Matthews, Chatto, ISBN: 0- 7011-3873-4 Covering the history of British film censorship, from the first banned film, which comprised a salacious piece of cheese, right up to the *Child's Play* press furore, this is a fascinating guide about one of horror's greatest challenges.

Nightmare Movies by Kim Newman, Harmony Books, ISBN: 0-517-57366-0 Kim Newman's passion for horror films is well known. This deals with horror and scary films by subject or subgenre (e.g. ghost stories, classical gothic, psycho movies) and covers a huge range of films. Special attention is given to such auteurs as Dario Argento, Larry Cohen, David Cronenberg and Brian De Palma.

Broken Mirrors Broken Minds: The Dark Dreams Of Dario Argento by Maitland McDonagh, Sun Tavern Fields, ISBN: 90-9517012-4-X *The* book about Dario Argento. It contains analyses of his films and an interview, filmography and reference section.

James Whale: A New World Of Gods And Monsters by James Curtis, Kevin Brownlow Faber and Faber; ISBN: 0571192858 A super biography of Frankenstein's cinematic creator.

Wes Craven's Last House On The Left: The Making Of A Cult Classic by David A Szulkin, F.A.B. Press This is not only an excellent guide to a notorious film, but also useful for learning about low-budget film-making.

Fearing The Dark: The Val Lewton Career by Edmund G Bansak, Robert Wise, McFarland & Company, ISBN: 089950969X Pricey and difficult to obtain, but a good guide to a fascinating producer.

Cronenberg On Cronenberg by David Cronenberg, Chris Rodley (Editor), Faber and Faber,ISBN: 0571191371 Another of Faber's series of interviews. Always recommended.

Others

There are so many horror books out there it is difficult to know what to recommend but a safe bet is anything by independent publishers Creation (83 Clarkenwell Road, London, EC1R 5AR) or F.A.B. Press (P.O. Box 178, Guilford, Surrey) both of whom have an eclectic range of specialised books for the horror aficionado.

Pocket Essentials

Yes, your favourite series of reference books come in more detailed flavours, all connected with horror. You might think brand loyalty compels us to mention these, but we have read (or written) every one and heartily recommend them.

David Cronenberg by John Costello, Pocket Essentials ISBN: 1-903047-26-9 Excellent guide that delivers the lowdown on Canada's most intelligent and disturbing director from shorts and obscure TV work to big budget features.

Slasher Movies by Mark Whitehead, Pocket Essentials ISBN:1-903047-27-7 All your favourite slasher flicks dissected for your enjoyment, plus a guide to surviving them should you ever need to...

Vampire Films by er, us, Pocket Essentials ISBN: 1-903047-17-X Vampires are the most malleable of movie monsters and this guide looks at early morsels right up to hi-tech Hollywood blockbusters, taking in vampires from around the world as well. A light guide to the creatures of the night.

John Carpenter by er, us again, Pocket Essentials ISBN: 1-903047-37-4 We just haven't had the space to write about one of the most respected of horror and science fiction directors and the man who has been such an important influence on the modern horror film. Discover all those missing gems right here!

Web Resources

Directors

Dario Argento: http://home2.swipnet.se/~w-20851/hemsida/dario.htm
Clive Barker: http://www.btinternet.com/~revelations/
Tod Browning: http://www.csse.monash.edu.au/~pringle/silent/ssotm/Jun96/
Wes Craven: www.wescraven.com
David Cronenberg: http://www.uncarved.demon.co.uk/2012/psycho.html
Joe Dante: http://eborisk.dusted.net/
Terence Fisher: http://www.icast.com/artist/1,4003,1010-249831,00.html
Val Lewton: http://www.acm.vt.edu/~yousten/lewton/
George A Romero: www.georgearomero.com
James Whale: http://www.sbu.ac.uk/stafflag/jameswhale.html

General

Hammer Films: www.hammerfilms.com
Troma Films: www.troma.com
Universal horror films: www.horroronline.com

Censorship

Censorship News (UK): www.melonfarmers.co.uk
UK Classification: www.bbfc.co.uk
US Classification: www.mpaa.org

Also Showing...

Space has limited the number of films we could discuss, but should you be seeking further scares and chills (with the odd chuckle) you could do a lot worse than the following:

The Cat And The Canary, Leni, 1927

Fall Of The House Of Usher, Epstein, 1928

Vampyr, Dreyer, 1931

Murders In The Rue Morgue, Florey, 1932

The Black Cat, Ulmer, 1934

The Spiral Staircase, Siodmak, 1946

House Of Wax, De Toth, 1953

Bucket Of Blood, Corman, 1959

The Innocents, Clayton, 1961

Carnival Of Souls, Harvey, 1962

Terror Of Dr Hitchcock, Freda, 1962

Dementia 13, Coppola, 1963

Onibaba, Kaneto Shindo, 1964

Multiple Maniacs, Waters, 1969

Blood On Satan's Claw, Hagard, 1970

The Devils, Russell, 1971

Hands Of The Ripper, Sasdy, 1971

Daughters Of Darkness, Kumel, 1971

Vampire Circus, Young, 1971

Death Line, Sherman, 1972

Blood Spattered Bride, Aranda, 1972

Don't Look Now, Roeg, 1973

The Wicker Man, Hardy, 1973

Deranged, Ormsby, 1974

Rocky Horror Picture Show, Sharman, 1975

Phantom Of The Paradise, De Palma, 1975

To The Devil A Daughter, Sykes, 1976

Alien, Ridley Scott, 1979

Phantasm, Coscarellli, 1979